Finding Prayer

J. H. Churchill

FINDING PRAYER

SCM PRESS LTD

334 00478 0

First published 1978
by SCM Press Ltd
58 Bloomsbury Street, London WC1

Typeset by Gloucester Typesetting Co. Ltd
Printed in Great Britain by
Fletcher & Sons Ltd, Norwich

CONTENTS

For Margaret

PREFACE

These chapters have been put together as a result of trying to help adults from a variety of walks of life and places to find their way into and on in prayer, either as individuals or in groups. After the shake-up in the sixties I found that I wanted to try to help people on a more empirical basis than was presented in some of the classical books. At the same time I wanted to help them share the classical experience and fields of prayer.

I originally conceived the work in two parts, but soon came to the conclusion that they must stand together; those who are finding their way into prayer see some further avenues opening up quite quickly, while others who are some way on in prayer often have to re-explore earlier areas. There are a number of books to help in various fields, some indicated at the end of this book – but few explore both the way in and the way on. This is offered as a short aid to that long exploration.

Carlisle
December 1977

J. H. Churchill

1 *Finding – The Way In*

'I don't know what you find in prayer.' This is the sort of comment or reflection often unspoken, made by the person who catches a friend at prayer. If the speaker puts it into words, he or she may go on to say 'I used to pray, but I never found I was getting anywhere. I suppose you find some comfort in it.' More wistfully, he may say 'when I do try to pray, I find that my mind keeps wandering off. More often, I simply can't find time to pray, yet somehow I find myself feeling guilty about it.'

The question of 'finding' keeps cropping up in the conversation or questions, spoken or unspoken, about prayer. So it may be useful to tackle the question of 'finding' prayer, though it is certainly not the only approach to the subject.

Behind the question of finding prayer, is the bigger question of whether we find God in our prayer. Directly you put it in this way, the further possibility arises that it is God who finds us, rather than we who find him. This possibility of course would not arise if God turned out not to exist, but then neither would the question of our finding God. Yet the question of God finding us still arises even when we ourselves wonder, or doubt, or deny, that God exists. He is still quite capable of finding us, though it may take rather longer for us to recognize him in that sort of situation. The same consideration applies when we think of God as remote, or impersonal, or unmoving; we are less likely to move towards him, but he may still move towards us.

There is a good deal of evidence, from all sorts of people, of all kinds of races and religions, that they have found God. In some religions there is also the sense of God finding, or meeting, us. This sense is more marked where God is seen to be personal and on the move, coming near; it is most clearly expressed in Christianity where men claim that God is to be found in the human life of Jesus, and in the continuous activity of the Holy Spirit at work in men and women. Two simple statements about finding God come from Christians of the fifth and eighteenth centuries. Augustine, the fifth-century Bishop of Hippo in North Africa, wrote in his *Confessions* 'Our hearts are restless till they find their rest in Thee.' In England in the eighteenth century, S. T. Coleridge wrote, in his aptly named *Confessions of an Inquiring Spirit*, 'Whatever finds me bears witness of itself that it has proceeded from a Holy Spirit.'

Coleridge's remark reminds us that different things can come home to us at different times, and to different people in different ways and degrees. Though Christianity has boldly claimed that God has shown himself in a particular and definitive way in Jesus Christ, most Christians by now have learned that this does not mean that he is not to be found in other religions. There is obviously a good deal of experience of God in the great religions of the East; their patient training in ways of finding God has brought new vision to many in the West, not least in this country in recent years. Yet it is noticeable that most Eastern religion is about our finding God by ways of clearing the mind, relaxing the body, contemplating nature. These methods may well help to bring some to the threshold, but that threshold has still to be crossed. The point of Christianity is that in Jesus, God has crossed that threshold to find us. This is the good news of the gospel. Coleridge's remark was, in fact, made in the course of his discussion of biblical inspiration. He was saying that we discover the truth of its inspiration, not in any extraordinary way, but in a simple experience of the way in which, through the Bible, God brings things home to us and really finds us. At the same time, Coleridge was very aware that God finds us through other things beyond the Bible.

The first point of Christian prayer then is that God finds us. There is much we can do to respond to this initiative; much thought and study has been given to this response down the ages. Nowadays, unfortunately, many Christians have forgotten, or never discovered, their own traditions of clearing minds, relaxing bodies, and learning to contemplate; they have a big gap in their understanding, which some now look to the East to fill. There is, however, much more immediate help at hand in our own Christian tradition. The trouble is that often prayer has been presented in one or other of fixed systems – a round of written prayers, or a particular use of the Bible, or a complicated ascetic training. The 'whatever' of Coleridge's remark points to the fact that God finds us, and we may find God in a variety of ways, and in a combination of these ways. For some, very obviously God is to be found in times of danger, when not a few turn to prayer, even in a casual ejaculation. Others turn to God in times of loneliness, or depression, or in failure and fault; somehow we feel responsible to him. We often look to him in our concern for others, maybe urgently for those near and dear, or complainingly for the world at large. Fortunately, too, there are moments when we turn to him in thankfulness, and realize how much there is in life for which to be thankful.

Beyond this gratitude we pass, at moments, into wonder. Yet we also wonder in another sense; we wonder whether he is there at all; we wonder what life is doing and what it means; we wonder also what we should do about it. These are not thoughts to be repressed, but to be explored. For it is only in looking that we find; it is only in being open to possibilities that we can discover that we have been found. It is always worth keeping ears, and eyes, and mind, open to look at life, to perceive, to feel the goodness, yes and the misery – to puzzle over the meaning and the mystery. It is worth bearing the responsibility and the pain of feeling for others, their needs, their hopes and fears; but we must also be prepared to look at ourselves, both at our gifts and our joys, and also our fears and failures, and at our questions and doubt too.

Somewhere amongst all these there is a way and ways to be found into prayer for most. If we only begin to investigate and to explore we shall find clues leading to further discoveries. If we are prepared to be open to new thoughts and the discovery to be made that God is reaching out to each one of us. There is another discovery to be made, that he is wanting to take us further than we realized. There are discoveries to be made in this process, in many different ways and many different times. We can look at a number of these ways, which do in fact all link up, but any one of them may be the way in for some person. If one proves to be a dead end, look on to the next. We may therefore start our investigations with a further look at 'wondering'.

2 *Wondering*

It is often in moments of delight and joy that we begin to wonder. There is much in which to delight in life, both in the splendours of nature, and the constructions of human ingenuity. Yet delight is not so easy when sun turns to rain, or skill to destruction. So we can wonder in a positive or in a negative way; we can wonder, at one moment, how marvellous life is, and then at the next wonder whether it is not too good to be true. In those moments of fear we need to shake ourselves and take in the joy of the present moment, and not to be afraid to live and delight in it. We need to recover our nerve. We often say this is the great need of the present age, but it has been very true of most ages. It is a great need of people.

In this need lies hidden the simple act of faith. Some in fact learn one kind of faith in recovery from illness, or from depression; this often entails faith in the help of a doctor or nurse. This then has to pass on to a faith in themselves, or a faith in life; it is a natural step on from this to faith in the goodness of life, and of people. This can prove to be a step towards faith in our Father. For others, this faith in life arises more easily from some vivid scene of beauty or an occasion of active goodness. It is there to be found, too, in the ordinary run of life, in the wonder of the daily round.

We can help ourselves to find this joy by stopping and looking at life. Often it requires a considerable effort to pause in a busy life and look at the world and people, as they rush by us and we rush by them. As W. H. Davies put it:

> What is this life, if full of care
> We have no time to stand and stare?

We need to give time to appreciate things and people; we all know how much we long for people to give us time, to attend to us, to speak to us, to appreciate us. We need to give ourselves time to attend to others, to appreciate them, and life, and God. The appreciation of people and God needs to be expressed in some form of gratitude, for through the things that they do and the things that happen to us, our life is sustained. There is a great field to explore, when we stop and look and appreciate; here is an avenue by which to find God, a way to appreciate his finding us.

The thought of appreciation points us to a further field, that of the arts. We learn to appreciate the beauty of form, of shape, colour, texture, maybe through painting, or dress, furnishing or architecture, or through music, drama or literature. Forms of beauty are indeed forms of life, not only in literature and painting, but also in architecture and music. It may well be that in listening to music, or looking at pictures, experiencing drama or literature, some find themselves wondering more and more, and gradually discovering new ranges of meaning. This can very well be a meeting with God, a way of finding him and being found by him. The understanding of life is enriched by these arts; through them we discover new meanings in life, new drama in it, new music, and we find ourselves appreciating further the richness of life and its author.

All these ways of wondering – and there are many others – contribute to the discovery that there is company in life, the company of the creator and the interpreter of life, God. If we stand and stare deeply, we can find the inside of life, and begin to appreciate something of God's point of view, or rather find ourselves invited to share in it. This is the experience which Christians came to call the fellowship or the communion of the Holy Spirit. These phrases are an attempt to express the sense that God communicates and shares with us his vision, his appreciation of life. Indeed, he communicates himself to us; he is prepared to go, step by step, with our slow pace, and the awareness of the finding on our part often comes very slowly. It did so with the first disciples, and has done so down the ages of the church where there have been very partial understandings and misunderstandings, mixed with great flashes of insight. This patience of God is all part of his goodness, his wonder, but it means we can be sure of his company from beginning to end.

Prayer indeed begins and ends in wonder; this may seem like a wistful hope to some, and a bad joke to others. The former can see, even from a distance, that if prayer works, it leads to the baffling wonder of communication with God Almighty. They are not mistaken; for this reason much of Christian worship, and indeed many Christian hymns, are concerned with praise. It is significant that the Sunday TV programme with a continual appeal is called 'Songs of Praise'; the name and the popularity bear witness to an important part of human experience.

The bad jokers also have a point. To them the possibility of communication with God would be a wonder indeed, and its pursuit even more unlikely. This thought is not to be lightly dismissed; on the other hand, it should not be accepted without further examination. This examination begins in simply wondering whether there is anything in this possibility of communication with God Almighty. The constructive step then is to explore such possibilities as lie to hand, and to see what there is available.

It is at this point that Christian experience in the New Testament has something very important to tell us. The men of the Old Testament had learned that Almighty God in his goodness was infinitely concerned with the men and women he had made. As Psalm 113 put it –

> Who is like unto the Lord our God, that hath his dwelling so high; and yet humbleth himself to behold the things that are in heaven and earth?

Yet the Jews had not, for the most part, bargained for the fact that God was prepared to become even more involved. Gradually, the men and women who followed Jesus of Nazareth discovered that in him God was participating in human life. This came out in a variety of impressions from supporters and opponents: 'No man ever spoke as this man speaks'; 'Who but God alone can forgive sins?'; 'You are the Messiah, the son of the living God'. These were half-impressions, unclear even to his supporters. They were all to be put into the melting pot by his death. 'We had been hoping that he was the man to liberate Israel' was the way the two men on the road to Emmaus put it.

Out of that melting pot the disciples found themselves confronted by the risen Jesus. This was no projection of their yearning imaginations; it was, in fact, contrary to their expectations. They did not recognize him at first; then they said, as it were, 'Of course. It is the Lord.' They needed reconvincing two or three times, so Mary Magdalene tried to cling to him, and doubting Thomas wanted to handle the scars. But when he was confronted by them, it was not surprising that his words were recorded as 'My Lord and my God'. For Thomas this was the end of what appeared to be a bad joke, when he had earlier said 'Let us go also, that we may die with him.' Through desperation and doubt Thomas came to find Jesus confronting him. The experience of the presence of the risen Christ did not end at this point, it only began there. These meetings were, in a sense, the completion of a relationship which has been remoulded in the melting pot, and which would give way to a more lasting experience of relationship.

We have a direct reflection of this experience of Christ's followers in Paul's letters. These are the oldest documents of the New Testament, written in the fifties of the first century, before the gospels took written form beginning with Mark's in the sixties. All the New Testament books are written in the common Greek of the day, yet both Paul's epistles and the gospels preserve a few words of Jesus in the actual Aramaic, the later form of Hebrew spoken at this time. 'Amen' is one familiar example, but a more significant one is 'Abba' or 'Father' in the form of speaking directly to one's father, the vocative case of the colloquial word. Joachim Jeremias has demonstrated from Jewish writings that Jews did not dare to address God in this way; only Jesus did so and those he taught.

This is in fact one of the great, if not *the* great, lesson of Jesus, that we can speak to God direct as Father. Furthermore, Paul tells us that Christians learnt that they could say this with real meaning. They had both Jesus' teaching in the Lord's Prayer and his example as the gospel records it in his prayer in the garden of Gethsemane; they had also their relationship with him in the Spirit. 'When we cry, Abba, Father', Paul wrote to the Romans, 'it is the Spirit himself bearing witness that we are children of God' (Rom. 8.15). He had written in the same vein to the Galatians 'Because you are sons, God has sent the spirit of his son into our hearts, crying "Abba Father", so through God you are no longer a slave but a son' (Gal. 4.6).

Christians claim from their experience that conversation with God is a real possibility. It is not by any kind of mystical conjuring trick, but through the goodness of God meeting men and women in Jesus, in getting across to them through his spirit, to bring them into a new relationship with himself. Prayer is the natural expression and articulation of this relationship. It is not to be thought of as an exotic exercise, nor even as a stern religious duty. It is being at home with God, our Father; it is a possibility he offers, but doesn't force, for our joy. The offer is always open. We can take a grip on ourselves and our fears, and move from a negative sceptical wondering to a positive exploration of the rich wonder of life. We can explore the delight of life through the appreciation of beauty and arts, and through attention to other people. We can find God coming to meet us in different ways. Christian evidence tells us that this need not be a fleeting experience. It is firmly based, both in what Jesus told us about 'our Father' and also in the way in which he staked his life on this relationship, and was raised, and enables his followers to continue in that relationship. We can find through him a way of being at home with God, so that we can begin to express and articulate our appreciation. It is not for nothing that Christians have often begun their prayer with the simple statement 'In the name of the Father, and of the Son, and of the Holy Spirit', and have ended it with the reminder from Paul 'The grace of Our Lord Jesus Christ, and the love of God, and the fellowship of the Holy Spirit.' Prayer begins and ends in wonder, the simple wonder of the goodness of life, opening into the deeper wonder of our relationship with God.

3 *Thanking*

Many of us spend some moments over the first sentence when we come to write a letter. How shall I begin? Often we are rescued from our dilemma by the simple fact that we can thank our correspondent for his or her letter. Though occasionally we have the difficult task of opening the correspondence, we are more often replying. In our communication with God we are always replying to the love and care, and outreach of God towards us that has been going on from his side from our birth. We never have to start this correspondence; we may need to wake up to its existence, but we are always replying, so we may then reasonably proceed by saying thank you.

Letter-writing reminds us that both with letters and prayers we are very slow to reply, and slow to say thank you. We are so taken up with our concerns and anxieties that it takes us some time to stop and wake up and say 'thank you'. When we do, we are overcome again by concern about our negligence and cut short our thanks and turn them into apologies. This has often happened with Christian prayer, both private and public. There is certainly a place in our prayer for saying sorry, but it is not normally the first place; there may be times when we are very conscious that we must start with it, but it is not the most natural opening. There is a great point in simply being thankful, and giving ourselves time to take in the goodness of life, and to appreciate it, and letting this appreciation grow.

There's plenty to be thankful about in life if we open our eyes to things and people, or to the beauty and interest in nature, gay and grim, or to the kindness and care of others. Then there are things which happen to us, and those which happen in us. We can savour all these and many others, and it's well worth doing so. Life has within it the possibility of delight and joy, and part of finding prayer and God is finding this delight. Look for the joy and delight, and find the thankfulness bubbling up.

We are often held back by that feeling that it's too good to last. Some have a sad suspicion that there must be a snag in the end, and others a deeper fear that good doesn't last but that evil persists. Both the suspicion and the fear need fighting. Both arise from an overconsciousness of self and lead us to look at the evidence in a prejudiced way; they can become neurotic flights from life, which turn us away from looking fairly at the evidence. At the beginning of the Bible you will find a good antidote to this thinking. Genesis was not the first book to be written; it was probably in their hard times in exile under Babylonian domination that the Jews retold and developed their creation stories. It is to their credit and to our continued blessing that those men had the vision to see through the struggles of life, typified by the element of chaos in the old myths, and to say beyond all this, 'In the beginning, God created.' They then went on to make the affirmation, at each stage of creation, 'God saw that it was good.' Belief in God, finding him behind life, is not a matter of finding an impassible first principle, or a colourless computer, but of finding the loving God who creates life good and sustains it.

Yet, when all that is said, we can't help being aware that much pain, and want, and injustice persist in the world. This is fair enough, and we must not waste that awareness, but act on it, though often we shall find that much of the action lies beyond our comprehension. We shall have to think further about caring, both in action and prayer later. Yet we shall care more and not less, and more effectively too, if we do not let this awareness cramp our thankfulness. In fact thankfulness can be the best spur and stimulus to caring. Many whose need or handicap invites our care, can teach us good lessons of thankfulness.

Those Jews who set out their belief in the good creator were well aware that there was much wrong with this fallen world. They drew on the old and subtle stores of men and women choosing their self-centred own way. They left us a vivid picture of the mixture of individual responsibility, the influence of one upon another, and the influence of those mysterious demonic forces, which spoke to their experience of wrong, and still speaks to ours. This is the Old Testament diagnosis in Genesis 3. To this the New Testament answers with the good news that in the life, suffering and death of Jesus of Nazareth, God himself has shared our situation. It says that in the resurrection we can both see the assurance of God's good and healing love, and also find the possibility of sharing in it. Like all good treatments, it involves participation by the patient; so the New Testament is well aware that there is much suffering and wrong in the world, and that it must await the final healing. Yet the fact of Jesus' suffering, and death, and resurrection, makes all the difference, both to the actual sufferer, and to us in our awareness of the continuing wrong in the world. Deep thanksgiving for this will help us to keep and not cover the awareness, but act and pray constructively. The General Thanksgiving rightly goes on from 'creation, preservation and all the blessings of this life' to 'redemption of the world by Our Lord Jesus Christ; for the means of grace, and for the hope of glory'.

The words of the General Thanksgiving may make some say that it's all very well thanking God when something good happens, but you can't thank to order, in prayer or in church. Others, however, will admit that the sonorous phrases of the General Thanksgiving, or of 'Now thank we all our God', stir them, not to any unreal emotion, but to a genuine gratitude. There is an obvious case for spontaneous thankfulness, but as in all sorts of activities, most of us need a good deal of training to be able to respond to life with real spontaneity. This is particularly true of gratitude, both in writing letters and in spoken thanks. We are all too aware that others often do not thank us when we expect them to do so; and we often resent this, yet our own experience ought to tell us that this is not so much from lack of awareness but from lack of practice. The person in practice is the one who can be spontaneous. This is true both about our thanksgiving to God in prayer, and also about other sorts of prayer.

It's worth stopping to thank God, in fact, each day. We can always find something to thank God for every evening. This is a step we can all take, if we only take the trouble to stop. In fact we can generally find three things to thank God for out of the morning, the afternoon and the evening. As we practice we can begin to look round and extend our view. We can move out from the pleasant things which happen to us, to some of the good going on around us, maybe affecting others more than ourselves. Then we can go on to see more in the things which happen to us but which may not strike us as so pleasant at the time. We gradually become grateful for all that is happening to us and in us, even what we are able to do ourselves. It's not proud to do this; in fact, thanking God is the best way to stop patting ourselves on the back.

Looking back, from the evening over the day, gives us just enough perspective to see below the surface, and to see something of what is going on in life. We can see more of this from the longer distance. Such further occasions for thanksgiving are given in the various seasons or moves in life; it may be an anniversary, or at the end of one job. It is good to look back, not just nostalgically but purposefully, and to see something of the detail of what God has given us in the meanwhile. Here again, practice helps us to rise spontaneously to such occasions.

Practice in longer and deeper thanksgiving is offered to us quite simply at the end of the week. Weeks are significant spans in most people's lives, more so than months. 'It's been a good week', or 'a disappointing one' we say. We are able to see through the disappointment to the underlying good, and to open eyes of gratitude; there is more to be found, we realize, as the days go by, more both in the disappointing and in the good weeks. We can see how things begin to build up and begin to take shape. It's interesting to note that the week has gripped man's imagination as a natural time to return specific worship to God, and thanksgiving has long been the basis of that act, from the earliest times. So it was at the week's turn, particularly, that Christians took up the command of Christ 'Do this in remembrance of me' in the breaking of bread. He himself had blessed and shared the bread and wine with the typically Jewish words of thanksgiving, so the title eucharist, or thanksgiving, has always marked the central act of Christian worship.

Thanksgiving lies at the heart of Christian corporate worship and personal prayer. It reflects the basic attitude of faith in and response to the loving father and the goodness of life. Furthermore, it takes us, as it were, into the inside of life. We begin to see something of what is happening to us and around us; we begin to see life taking shape. We think not only of God's loving hand, but also of the wonder that he allows us to have a share in the shaping of life. There is a fascinating and encouraging field to explore here; the steps into that field are very natural and simple; they are certainly steps towards finding God, and seeing something of what he is doing. They are familiar steps; anyone can take them who will stop and look and think and thank, any night, any week, any year.

4 *Thinking*

It is not always obvious which is the simplest way to climb a mountain. The full face, which gives the most imposing view, is not normally the easiest to climb. You need to look for ridges, and this often means ridges behind other ridges, and you have to find your way round by these. It is like this for many people with public buildings; there may be an imposing main entrance, but that looks too big for us to enter alone, so we generally work round to find some side door for our modest entrance. So it is with God: the full face is in many ways an arduous climb. The grand entrance may be opened to us sometimes, when we are caught up in a great act of public worship; on our own we often have to look round and find one point that leads to another. We need, in fact, to do some thinking point by point.

We may have to begin this process of thinking round the very question as to whether there is the possibility of some sort of conversation with God. We may cover some of the foreground and get over some of the obstacles to a clear view by seeing that listening to God is, in a sense, picture language, but nonetheless useful. It is said that only the very holy, or the very simple, or perhaps the very over-wrought people are likely to hear something like voices. However, in any conversation, the important part is the ideas that are exchanged, and so it is with God. But it is important, in an exchange of ideas that there should be some genuine reception, of which listening is the best picture. It is also necessary that we should go on to try and understand the ideas or what we hear, so receptiveness and understanding will be important parts of our attempt to explore relationship or conversation with God.

Listening can be thought of in both an active and a passive form. There is a way of positive attention, with an active effort to understand; there is also a passive way of taking in what comes over to us, and letting it sink in and make an impression on us, so that the point gradually becomes clear. We often find ourselves oscillating between these two ways. We find our interest aroused by a chance impression, something we see or something we hear, and then we turn and try to find out more. On the other hand, it may well be that we are trying to find our way into some matter and to understand it properly, but find our minds running round in a circle; we are baffled. We do well then just to let the matter circulate in our mind and gradually find one or two major points come to the surface, and we find that we can begin to see and understand clearly.

So it may be with God. We can find the way into conversation with him by thinking, both actively and passively. We have already seen some avenues to explore by way of wondering and thanking. Through these we can see that there is much to set us thinking in the mystery of life, and there is a deal of good to set us thanking. In both these ways we begin to see that there is indeed something 'going on' in life. We begin to appreciate God's point of view and activity, and to enter into it. It's worth, in fact, letting the impression of wonder and thankfulness sink in, and giving some thought to them; this gives a chance for God's point of view to become clearer to us and engage us, and draw us into conversation. We may discover that God is even more interested in this possibility than we are and we find a gentle encouragement and urge to look further with him.

There are all sorts of impressions of life that can set us thinking, not only those which more obviously set us wondering and thanking. It may well be the way in which a person says or does this or that; it's worth noticing these things, and pondering them for a moment. Then there are certain experiences; some of these make a very vivid impression at the time, others we only notice as we look back on them. Yet in such moments we see life in depth, as it were 'in stereo', and find it saying something to us. These are times to attend, to think, to listen, and find God presenting things to us quietly, but calling for our attention, and though it may take us a long time to realize it, calling for our response. These times are not so rare as we may imagine; once we open up our ears and minds to take in the ordinary impressions of life, these are there to savour, not only the beautiful countryside, but as much in the crowded, humdrum world of the street, the factory, the kitchen. It is well worth trying to look, and to listen, and to try to understand.

It's this kind of attention that gave the writers of the Bible their insights into God's activity; certainly they were often looking at particular events in the life of the Jewish nation, and more particularly in the life of Jesus of Nazareth, yet they looked at these by looking at the ordinary things of life around them, sometimes directly and sometimes indirectly. So the prophets looked at the politics and the social issues of their time, and the disaster of their nation, and could see God's activity at work even in the heathen conqueror. At other times they looked indirectly, and Jeremiah learnt from the blossom of the almond tree, or from the work of the potter at his wheel, to look for God. We know, too, that Jesus taught his disciples to look at a woman searching for a lost coin in the dust, or a swindling bailiff doing some quick thinking, to learn about God, and response to him. He taught men to look at the seed time and harvest, and the red sky at night, and learn to look at what was happening in the world, and the need to think and act upon it.

In all sorts of ways the Bible encourages us to look hard at life and to think hard and purposefully. It may be that we are pointed in a direct way to look at a crisis situation, or it may be that we are encouraged to look in a more reflective way of reviewing the way men and nature work, the way things look. In one way or another Jesus called men to look and understand and make up their minds, 'Why can you not judge for yourselves?' he said. His followers found that they began to see, and to see more, after he had died, and risen, and left them; they found that he had left them with his spirit, and as he had promised, that spirit really worked to help them to understand his mind.

We can find this in ourselves. Looking, and thinking, can lead us to discover something of what God is doing and saying in life. It will help to open our minds to the possibility that the spirit of God can show us something, and not least help us to share something of the mind of Christ.

It's not only those who are familiar with the gospels, but those who come to them afresh, or who turn back to them after having dismissed them, who find that they do present particular opportunities to see and understand something of depth in life. Jesus, in a remarkable way, made men, and still makes men, concentrate attention on the issues of life. He, as it were, puts his finger on the spot. Looking attentively at particular incidents and passages in the gospels is one of the simplest ways to understand the particularity of Christ, to begin to see why people make such claims about him. But we don't have to form any conclusions about the claims to practise this looking in an expectant way at those vivid scenes in the gospels. You can look both at those where Jesus is doing something direct, and also at those pictures that Jesus drew in parables. The gospels mostly fall into short, vivid paragraphs, which have a fairly clear point, often made in a punch line. This witnesses to the fact that the gospels were put together from material that was passed on by constant re-telling in the early church with a point to help see what Jesus was getting at, what sort of person he was. So they provide us now with eminently suitable material and units to look at, and to think about. It is not too difficult for us to find them coming alive or alight for us, and in this way to discover that the spirit of God does open things up for us. It's worth noting Jesus' constant insistence on action, even though we may only get there at the second or third attempt. The illumination that comes out of an incident in the gospel is likely, therefore, to carry some applications for action. It is worth looking and thinking about these implications; they may be big at times, or small, or more general at others.

We can see that process of the Spirit at work lighting and enlivening men and women in the first generation of the church, in the Acts and the epistles, or letters in the New Testament. Never forget that Paul's letters were written before the gospels. The letters give us fascinating evidence of the impact on the first generation. They may seem strange to us in some ways, but in a modern translation it becomes clear to us that they are letters of a real man writing about real questions concerning both the world and God. He writes often much more starkly than we dare to think. Incidentally, they make clear to us that if we want to find our way through thinking about the New Testament it is important to read it in a modern translation, and to see that it is concerned with real people in our real world.

It is also important to remind ourselves again that it is not just from the New Testament that we can find our way into this looking, listening and thinking. The New Testament itself springs out of the depth of life, and makes us to look into those depths; in fact it encourages us to look in depth into the life around us. We can think about the run of the day. It's worth going on beyond thinking about its effect on us, and whether we get things done or not, and try to think about it as it happens, and gradually see that the meetings of life, both chance and arranged ones, and many of the pieces of work that fall our way, have some real significance. Through them we can gradually begin to see that something is really happening around us in life, it's not a meaningless round but an event in which we have a chance to participate.

This is true, too, when we look at still life. We see things which in themselves make us think, and see something of the individuality of things. This again invites us to see our individual part in the whole. If we stop and think, we have a chance to find a remarkable depth, to find the life below the surface, and a call to us, in our depth and individuality, to respond and participate. This is the way in, to find God in the midst of life, and his invitation to us to share it with him.

This moving and still life, is, of course, the particular field of writers. We often first begin to see something of the worth and moods of life as we get interested in the threads of a novel, or in its descriptive passages. We may find ourselves invited to look in depth at some person or thing by a poem. Both invite us a little further on in that journey into life, which will lead us to find God. It's worth, therefore, giving ourselves the opportunity both to read and to muse about our reading of all sorts of literature.

Getting to know God is immensely worthwhile; in fact it is worth everything, like the pearl of great price in the gospels. So it is worth using everything – thinking, musing, novels, poetry, Bible and musing again. The more we get to know God, the more we find he is inviting us to share his mind and his activity. We can see that he leaves us free to share or not, he invites both questions and response, but he certainly invites us to understand, and much of our further explorations into asking and sharing God depend on this growing understanding. So it's well worth giving attention to the thinking, to stop, and look, and listen, and understand.

5 *Asking*

Some may well have found what has gone before too roundabout and too indefinite – beating about the bush, evading the issue. For the issue of prayer for them is asking, asking God for things. For such people the great question is what answers, if any, do we get to our prayers?

The question is a multiple one; it may be put in an objective way, as to whether we can achieve results in prayer, get things done, change the world. It may be asked more subjectively; does God answer requests, does he in fact say yes, or maybe no, to you and me? Very often it means, can we get a specific answer to the particular question as to what we are to do or to say. Can we, in fact, find guidance? When they are set out like this these questions look crude. They are crude, but nonetheless, or rather all the more, they are a real part of the crude stuff of human life, and woe betide us if we are too sophisticated to reckon with that stuff.

It's clear from the gospels that Jesus was well aware of the basic stuff of human life, and had to work and speak to it. He met people where they were in prayer, and said 'Ask and you will receive; seek and you will find; knock and the door will be opened.' Here is a very real encouragement for those who claim that the commonsense way of asking is the real way into prayer. It certainly is a way in, as many have discovered, in times of crisis. All the same, it may be worth noticing that the gospels do not put these as Jesus' first words on prayer; both in Luke and Matthew they come after Jesus' specific teaching on prayer given in the words of the Lord's Prayer. It is interesting to note that Luke said this teaching was given in response to the disciples' request for help in finding their way in prayer. We might take this as a hint that one of the first things to ask God for in prayer is for help to pray.

All the same, it is important to listen carefully to the answer to this request for help that Jesus gave. Many people seem to plunge headlong into the Lord's Prayer, only to surface in its later stages at 'Give us this day our daily bread – forgive – deliver'. They feel that there is straight asking if you like. Yes, but if you reflect, the earlier requests asked 'Thy kingdom come, thy will be done, on earth as in heaven.' This is very reasonable; the one-sided conversation of asking, one-sided pouring out of needs and troubles, soon palls. We tend to avoid people who do this to us. For genuine conversation there must be some genuine interest in the other person. Our Father asks for our interest in his will and kingdom. Once this begins to sink in on us, all our asking has to be in that context.

There are further surprises in store here, as there were for the first disciples. They thought that Jesus would demonstrate God's work with a military kingdom, a display of force and power. They were amazed to find that he was heading for a way of suffering, and was prepared to bow to the fate of death. Jesus himself knew how baffling this way was. Though he had committed himself to it long since, he felt the deep difficulty, and he was prepared to ask for himself 'Father, take this cup from me', as he faced the prospect of suffering and death. But he was ready, too, to pray as he taught others, and to continue 'Yet not what I will, but what Thou wilt.' Jesus' words come full circle. Yes, asking is a great way into prayer, but asking God must involve a concern for God's way, and that way, Jesus tells us, involves being prepared to co-operate with and to trust God's way, even to the point of death. The way into prayer by asking needs thinking about. Thinking can lead us to a very commonsense consideration about the danger of Christians trying to manipulate God. It can give us an opportunity to stop and begin to take notice of God himself, and to take an interest in him. It can give us an opportunity to look for some help in finding out what he wants. These things often present us with a clash between our own inclination and his will, and between our rather tentative efforts to do his will and the strong pressure of a world busy organizing itself to please itself.

Asking is, for many, the most immediate way into prayer. It is immediate in another way; it tips you straight into the big questions of dealing with God. Those two brothers, James and John, put the request that we all want to make at times, in their words to Jesus in Mark 10.35, 'Master we should like you to do us a favour.' Jesus quickly asks them what they mean, and they have to admit they want the best places in his kingdom. Jesus at once faces them with the necessary qualifications 'You do not understand what you are asking. Can you drink the cup that I drink, or be baptized with the baptism with which I am baptized?' It may appear to us a difficult theological reply, but the difficulty really is of another kind. It's not hard to see that he is warning them that they will have to share his way of suffering, even death; that's more than they bargained for.

This gospel incident points the matter in a stark and compressed way; for most of us it is more drawn out. James and John may encourage us by showing us that asking favours of God is no new thing. They can also help us to look through our apparently polite advances, and to ask what we really want. God, long before the caseworkers, wants to help us to insight about our deep desires. He wants us to express them, and in the expression begin to come to some understanding. He wants us to begin to see what our wants involve, and to work on step by step, to see more and more. Even from that compressed gospel incident you can see that Jesus' answer to the request is not a quick, expendable favour, in the fashion of a modern free offer, but a much more generous offer of involvement and sharing with him.

The answer to our asking may well be the beginning of an awareness of the work we need to do. This may come in a simple way to us when we ask for some advance or success, and only gradually come to realize that we must work to become better qualified. There may be a further realization that we should work for the sake of others, to be more useful and not just more comfortable, yet to find, in this process, we are more deeply happy. It's only in looking back that people begin to see that an answer has been worked out. They can look back and see that they were very worked up about something, so that they even tried praying about it. Then somehow they seemed to cool down a little, and look round, and realize they had better do this or that about it. This realization may have come only slowly, and with difficulty, and yet gradually they have found themselves working for something, instead of being just worked up about it. This is all part of the way in which God calls us to participation, for he won't manipulate us, and we have to learn not to try to manipulate him.

This gradual process of awareness doesn't mean either that prayer is ineffective or that God is telling us not to be so impudent or lazy as to ask. No, God is not rejecting in this way, rather this is his way of drawing us into a more thinking relationship. 'What is it you want?', 'Can you drink the cup?' Again, long before the caseworkers, he wants to help us into participation, to do our part, to find out what we need to do. He wants to enable us to meet the difficulties and the disappointments which we are very likely to encounter. Jesus didn't tell James and John that they couldn't share his cup, he said they would, and in different ways they did. All the same, he had to prepare them to face the fact that they couldn't pick and choose their own status and positions, as we so often expect to. A whole lot of our asking is really about having life according to our own choosing, yet we have only to reflect for a moment on the way we react to people around us who are always wanting things according to their choosing. We are always wishing that those people would wake up and grow up. We ought to wish and pray this for ourselves; here, indeed, is something to ask about. With those other people we tend to alternate between haughtily putting them in their place and then wearily giving way to them. God is humbler and firmer. He helps us gently to become aware that we are not the only pebbles on the beach, and that we just can't have everything our own way.

There is much more to learn, of course. There is the whole extension of this self-concern, fear and greediness across the world. We should not be surprised that things don't work out smoothly, that there is so much injustice and inhumanity, or that suffering falls on the innocent as well as the guilty. Though it is a natural reaction of our self-preservation to react against suffering, once we start to reflect we shouldn't be surprised that it occurs. We may need to remind ourselves once again that God does not manipulate people, and therefore he doesn't wrap us up in cotton wool to isolate us from suffering, for that would be to cut us off from relationships and life. This doesn't mean that we just sit down under suffering – a conclusion which has been falsely drawn by Christians and others at certain periods. Here again, prayer is likely to sharpen our awareness of our responsibility, even to deal with our own misfortunes. We shall find the responsibility both to care for those who suffer misfortune, and those who cause it; we must go on to think more about this care.

There is a need, too, to grow in the awareness of the fact of death. We are beginning to be aware today of the conspiracy of silence of doctors, relatives and patients about death. It is no ultimate help to any of them. We have often encouraged this conspiracy in prayer, yet in asking God for help we are likely to be led to insight, to sharing, to discipleship. You may find that the most urgent prayers in the face of impending death are likely to be met with a growing awareness and a chance to come to terms with it, a chance for the patient, the relative and probably the nurse. Furthermore, with Jesus, death and for that matter all suffering, can be a time to find that the answer to prayer lies in a closer company with him. We can know that he has been this way before, and shares it with us now, and in this way does his work of redeeming the pain and failure in the world, and we are invited to share this with him. This is indeed something to ask, and to receive.

6 *Caring*

Asking for ourselves may be all very natural, but it must be somewhat suspect, so we feel, at any rate, in our more altruistic moments. Many people would want to shift the ground rapidly and say 'When I think of prayer, I think of asking for other people.' They would say the important question to answer was whether praying for others is really effective or not. Those who ask this question, are threatened by negatives from two directions. First there is the answer of those who say bluntly that prayer doesn't do anything at all. The second answer, from those who say 'You don't want to pray for others, you want to do something positive to help them.'

This last answer begs the question as to whether prayer may not be one of the most positive things we can do for others. Yes, one of the things, because the full answer is that when we pray for others we often ought also to act for them in other ways. Indeed, if we have been right in thinking that asking God opens up a conversation with him in which he will be helping us to insight and to participation, then praying for others is likely to lead us to face the need for action on behalf of them. As when we ask for ourselves, so when we ask for others, we may take some time to wake up to our responsibilities. Yet it is not too difficult to see the need for action.

Yet acting on behalf of others raises plenty of questions too, and we are as slow to see these as we are the questions raised by praying for others. However, we are quick to notice the difficulties presented by the actions of others. We complain that they cheerfully go on doing things without asking themselves any questions. We have even made a rude phrase of 'do-gooder', to describe such people. When we try to do good for others we need to ask deep questions – Is this really for their good, or just for our own ideas about their good? Is the action, in fact, really for our own self-satisfaction? Generally, we have to face the fact that our motives are always mixed. There is bound to be some self-satisfaction in our action, but we still need to act for others. More seriously, we need to try to get clear what is really for their good and not just for our idea about it.

Further questions are opened up. Can we know or do what really needs doing? Can we see all that is involved? It is not long before we see that there is a whole lot beyond us. This becomes clear as soon as we get involved in a close personal issue such as a friend's broken marriage, or when we look into a big issue such as some conflict of race. We know we must do what we can, but can see there is much beyond us, and much that is uncertain. As we look into the questions about action, we find ourselves reaching into them in prayer. Certainly, praying for others will lead us to acting for others, but equally, acting for others in any deep way will lead us back to praying for them.

At the same time, we don't want to become 'do-gooders' in prayer, or 'naggers' of God. Praying for others isn't a matter of worrying with God, though it is all too easy to turn it into that. It is a matter of sharing care with him. For ourselves care in the sense of anxiety, needs to be seen in the context of taking God and both his care and will seriously; so our care for others needs to be set in the context of taking God and his care for them seriously. This step of reaching out in care for others is, in effect, a step of faith, albeit hesitant. Many, in fact, take this step without realizing it, at the bedside of a child or some other relative or friend, when they pray and, indeed, trust God. They may feel that they have little faith, but what they have they offer, like that father in the gospel, with the epileptic son, who said, in the poignant words 'Lord I believe, help thou my unbelief' (Mark 9.24).

Incidentally, the parent at the bedside, along with many of us in practice, gives the answer to our more sophisticated questions

'Ought we to pray for others? Isn't it manipulating God? Isn't it unfair on those who have no one to pray for them?' The answers lie in the thoughts we have already had. We must care for others, beyond even what we can do for them by direct action. We need to reach out further, we need to trust them to God and share our care with him, or rather share God's care for them. The Bible is full of the sense that God cares and loves much more widely than we do. Also it shows us that God shares his creative love with us. This is part of what is meant by creation in the image of God, that men and women have freedom and power to act and to co-operate with God or not, to help or not, to pray or not.

The New Testament fills this out further. Jesus taught his disciples to pray, and more than that called them to pray with him in that urgent hour in Gethsemane. They came to understand that his whole life of teaching, his acts of healing, and also his suffering and death, were all part of a great act of care for the world and the commitment of it, in trust, to his Father. It was all, his great act of prayer. They feared this had all come to nothing, but the resurrection showed them God's acceptance and vindication of it all from the other side of death. They saw this as the complete acceptance by the Father, so that Christians came to think of Jesus as sharing all the cares and concerns of humanity with his Father, and also still sharing life with his fellow human beings. He is, indeed, the great go between, the great intercessor, and both Paul, in the letter to the Romans, and the unnamed writer of the letter to the Hebrews, described Jesus as ever living to make intercession for us (Heb. 7.25; cf. Rom. 8.34). The formula at the end of the church's prayers 'through Jesus Christ Our Lord', is no arbitrary signal to the congregation to say 'Amen'; it is, indeed, the basis on which Christians see their prayer working. Prayer is sharing care with God as revealed in Jesus Christ, who has gone through suffering and death, and is alive for evermore, sharing our care with his Father, and sharing his care with us through the Holy Spirit.

This sharing of care with Christ can help our prayer in all

sorts of ways. We've already taken note of direct encouragement 'Ask and you shall receive'. We see that this has to be taken along with the Lord's Prayer – 'Thy will be done, thy kingdom come'. We can ask boldly all right but we must relate our prayer for others, either individually or corporately to the expression of God's rule or kingdom in the world. Does this or that prayer for that person or that group really further God's rule, or is it, in fact, trying to wrap them up in cotton wool and insulate them from God's will in the world? We need to stop and ask this question at times. Certainly the Lord's Prayer reminds us to pray not only for individuals but also for groups and indeed for organizations, and for the wide issues of the world. We mustn't treat the wide issues or institutions as outside God's concern. It is often harder to hold these in our minds, but the issues of the moment come up and focus them for us.

All that we have thought about not getting our way, about the facing of disappointments, suffering and even death, applies to our prayer for others as well as to our prayer for ourselves. There are a number of further considerations to be borne in mind when we try to pray about people in groups and great causes. We become more and more aware that we have our responsibility. We become very aware that we work in a world much bigger than ourselves, which makes demands beyond our limited possibilities. It's all the more important then to know that we share this work with Christ, who has worked in this wider world. He has worked within human limitations, both those imposed by his own physical strength and those imposed by the blindness and folly of others.

We can use the firm basis of his life and death and resurrection to spell out this sharing. One simple way to do this is to set out our concern for others alongside the concern shown by Jesus in some particular scene in the gospels. This may be done by simply recalling some passage or actually reading it over. We have already looked at one anxious parent in the gospel; there are others to be found amongst families and friends, alongside the sick. We can put our concern alongside those men who carried their paralysed friend to Jesus; we notice their determination as they pulled up the roof to get their friend to him. His first response may surprise us, as it did them, that response of forgiveness, only to be followed by the healing later. But this gives a good deal to work on. We can bring some of the hungry people of the world alongside the feeding of the five thousand, and we might do well to read in St John's version, in chapter 6, and go on to the end of the chapter, and pick up some points from that gospel's reflection on the feeding 'The bread that I will give is my flesh for the world.' Such reflections may help us to face the deep issues that lie under the problems of hunger and distribution in the world.

The feeding of the five thousand gives us another line of help, with that remark that Jesus looked at the crowd as sheep having no shepherd. This can remind us that it's not so much a matter of our sharing our cares with him, but of trying to share his care. We learn from the gospel to look with him at the crowd, as it were over his shoulder. The gospel suggests to us some significant moments of his looking – at the hungry crowd, from the boat on the lakeside beaches, and not least from the cross. We can also catch something of his care as he looked at individuals, and again there are some significant figures – an anxious parent, a rich young man, a Peter and a Judas. Using these gospel passages need not be just an exercise in imagination, it can give us a demanding way to exercise our mind and will, and to get us on the way to actions. It sets us on the way of doing this not alone but with him, with Christ, and therefore prepared to face his way of dealing with disappointment, difficulty, even downright failure. Yet he called his disciples to share prayer with him, and he calls us to participate too. He promised them that they would do great things after his death and resurrection, as they shared in the life of the Spirit, both in prayer and action, and indeed, in suffering; so our sharing will be sometimes in prayer, sometimes in action, sometimes in suffering, either in the direct form or the indirect form of disappointment.

Though we do well to stop at times, and to turn deliberately to particular passages in the gospels, to share the care of Christ, at other times we have got to move more quickly. We can quite fairly pray for individuals or groups or causes in one sweep. We can express our care and share with Christ in trusting to our Father. It's a help to remember that the hard facts of Jesus' life and death and resurrection, and the experience of Christians down the ages, lie behind the phrase 'Through Jesus Christ, Our Lord'. They can give us an understanding and a picture of the intercession of Christ – his going between the world and God – so that our modest thought of people and causes is part of something much greater.

We can begin to see more of this being part of something greater when we share our care visibly with others. This may grow out of some common piece of work, or a special effort to get something done, whether it be constructing a building or launching some social effort. It may be a piece of continuing work in which we all share as colleagues in a works, an office, a hospital, or the common responsibility we have, say as parents; in a group we may be bolder to realize there is much more in a task than meets the eye, and someone may be bolder still to suggest praying about it. It may be simply that this spurs people to pray on their own, encouraged by the thought that others are doing the same. Others will find it better to try to express their prayer together. Others still will want to do it by joining in some common act of worship. Others still will never be so fortunate as to find a close group where they can share this care. Though they can be sure there will be other people caring somewhere, they can begin to realize that they share the care with Christ through the Spirit, and are indeed never alone. The responsibility for others of itself can help us to see that we share this care with Christ, and with others who also care. The bonds of human responsibility are very real, and open us up to one another and to God, and this is certainly a real way in to explore.

7 *Sharing*

It is often easier to do things with others, 'I will, if you will.' 'I don't think I can do it on my own.' These are familiar remarks made for a variety of reasons. They may be dictated by the sheer size of the task, or by the weight of responsibility, by the need of company or by the alarm of self-consciousness. These remarks are common enough with young people, but are not uncommon with adults, particularly when we are trying something for the first time.

When we are able to share things with others we generally find an increase in effectiveness. This isn't only an increase in mechanical effectiveness, whether of body or mind, but there is often a greater understanding and depth in the work derived from the exchange of ideas and the difference of viewpoints. So we may take steps to facilitate the co-operation by clear instructions or to improve the rhythm by music, and to promote the exchange by consultation.

The work of finding God is helped by sharing too. Though much of it must be done on our own, and people vary in the ease with which they share deep things, it is safe to say that all are helped by some sharing in one way or another. Here self-consciousness may work in more than one direction. Some will find the thought of sharing the search for God with others causes them to blush at the very idea. Others, even these very same people, will be waiting to be helped by a gentle friend to take the first step of introduction to the friendship of God; here we return to the thought that God is not inactive, he moves to meet us.

God is, in fact, reaching out to us in the Spirit, in what the New Testament calls 'the fellowship of the Holy Spirit'. Indeed, he often finds us through other people, in our families, amongst our friends, in the company of the church. This doesn't mean that the finding is secondhand, or second rate; it's all of a piece with the experience of the men in the New Testament, who found God afresh through Jesus, and found that they could only fully understand God in relationship. They found that Jesus went on relating to them through the intimate activity of the Spirit, but he also linked them one to another, in the very real fellowship or sharing of the Spirit. This sharing is the reason for the church, both of its birth and of its being, in truth its *raison d'être*. This sharing in life with God through the Spirit is certainly not confined within the four walls of church buildings, or to the membership lists of the churches. It crops up in all sorts of places; in all sorts of manners of sharing you can find relationship with God in prayer, in the fellowship of the Spirit. No way is exclusive, and no list exhaustive. We can look through a few possibilities, and these may suggest others.

The sharing of a piece of work gives a basic sense of common humanity; people on a job soon become friends. Through what often begins as common pride in the job, we may begin to get a sense of sharing in taking a hand in some little piece of creativity. We can experience this in all sorts of work, whether it is a tough piece of physical effort, or a long mental process of struggling with a common problem, whether it is a complex commercial concern or organizing a piece of service. This sense may become more vivid when we can take a real interest in the object of the work, particularly if it is one we have had a share in choosing, and one which we can see helps others. If we don't get much chance to do these things in daily work, sharing in some piece of voluntary work may be a simple way of beginning to experience this sharing in creativity and working with others and with God. It need not surprise us if we find ourselves feeling this in an instinctive way through the simple satisfaction of physical effort and the enjoyment of others' company. We are asked to worship God with all our strength, and this may be a very real way in which we respond to our Creator through Christ who shared in human work in the fellowship of the Spirit.

We may well find that nothing much of this registers with us. We may feel that it is only when we begin to know others, and can talk and exchange ideas with them that we begin to get somewhere. Here we find the help of seeing things from different viewpoints, and experience the sympathy and understanding of others and the opening out of ourselves. We begin to find we are looking further into things. The dynamics of a group, which have been studied so much in recent years, give us a great opportunity to grow in sensitivity, in awareness of other people and of ourselves. What is not always recognized is that the dynamic life of a group gives us the opportunity to become more aware of God at work in other people and in ourselves, and to become more sensitive to his invitation to us to share in his concern and work. So it may be that some talking in a fortuitous gathering of friends, may leave us thinking, and indeed yearning. This is well worth noticing and extending. We look for an opportunity to talk further with that or another group. We may in fact arrange some sort of group. As this talking stimulates our sensitivity to the point of yearning we shall find ourselves on the edge of prayer.

It may be that an invitation to share in prayer is just what is needed for someone to get through the barrier of self-consciousness to find prayer, and at one time we may be at the receiving end and at another at the giving end of this invitation. A silence kept together may be a very real way of sharing. If we have begun to see the real possibility of finding God in prayer, and of his finding us, it is a great strength for us to wait with others in silence on God. Silence is not negative and need not be awkward. It can be a great relief and a very positive waiting on God. The Society of Friends has made this the backbone of its worship and life. Yet even the Friends have to combine silence with speech, if they are to live and work together, and after the silence they know all the more clearly the responsibility and the difficulty of speaking. So we may find ourselves feeling our way towards some sharing in prayer through words. Most likely it will be by discussing some common concern for which we want to pray: it may help both to give the prayer a base and ourselves a start, if we find some passage in the gospels as a background. On this it is not difficult to gather the concerns of the various members of the group, by someone collecting them up, or all throwing them in, and then caring in simple silence.

For most of us life cannot be lived in silence or in small groups. We have to relate to others in the larger units in work, our shopping, and in living in all sorts of ways, so part of finding God in his whole relationship with us will only be found when we look for him in the larger group of the church. In the church we can share both in the neighbourhood group of the local church, and through its common faith and heritage in national and international groups. Indeed we all gain some help on the way to finding God in Christ from the corporate life of the church through our dependence on the scriptures, which the church has put together and passed on. It was the corporate experience of the first Christians which fashioned the actual text of the gospels, as well as the letters of the New Testament, just as the corporate experience of Israel made the Old Testament. It is the corporate experience of Christians down the ages that has given us not only our church and its ministry today, but also our Christian education and the Christian ethos we find, all mixed up with other things, in our culture.

These reflections may remind us how much we need a corporate background and expression for our thinking and living, so it is not surprising that many drop into a church service and find themselves joining in the common expression of faith even in spite of themselves. It may well be by dropping into the back of a congregation anonymously and picking up the old hymns and prayers, that we can most easily find our way to God for the first time, or back to him. It is certainly one of the ways he finds his children, and the way he sends children older in the faith to find others. Of course there is much more to be found in Christian worship than that; the services are not just emotional dramas, though they may have both drama and emotion. They are not just a succession of mantras or words to assist concentration in prayer, though services certainly are an assistance to prayer, but prayer is conscious relation to the personal God. So Christian worship is basically response to what God has shown us in the particular revelation in Christ. It is therefore built round the scriptures applied in preaching, and the specific acts Christ gave us in his sacraments. By these he enables us to share his actions with him, self-giving in worship to the Father and in service to men. So there is plenty to think about in Christian worship, and it's well worth asking and reading about it. We need to learn to participate or share in its performance. Worship calls us to pray but also to act. We begin to pray in action in our worship – in standing, kneeling and sitting, speaking, singing, listening – and it may involve more than this, shaking hands, going up to altars, eating, drinking.

The action doesn't end there. Christian worship is meant to issue in the acting congregation. We ought to get to know the people we worship with, we ought to go and think and talk and act with them. In the process of doing this we go back through the ways we have looked at of sharing in action with others, ways which open us further to finding God. These ways all link up; one will open up for one person and another for others and we can go in through any of them. All these ways are open to us to share with others, in work, in the neighbourhood, in church, to find the fellowship of the Spirit, to find God.

8 *Turning*

'He needs to mix with other people.' 'He needs the corners knocking off.' 'She needs drawing out of herself.' So we venture to prescribe for other people, particularly those younger than ourselves. We recognize that people need changing, and are hopeful that contact with others will effect this. Perhaps this is a backhanded way of admitting that we have been changed by mixing with others; we have had our corners knocked off; we have been drawn out of ourselves, though we didn't like to admit it at the time. Our neighbours have been glad of this, and later we begin to see the benefit.

Certainly we gain a great deal from relationships with others; it may be a particular person whom we admire, a friend, or a wife or husband. It may be from a group of colleagues at work, or from a group that we seek out. We are challenged by their demands, both those expressed in their remarks, and others implied in their relationship to us. We are stimulated by their thoughts and their examples to adopt new attitudes. We may learn to look wider, and to rise to new heights. We are even more touched by the concern other people show for us, and respond to their interest and love. We warm up, we come out of ourselves; so we are gradually drawn out, changed. We are in fact turned inside out from our over-interest in ourselves and our self-consciousness and begin to look out to other people, to show some concern for others and to reach out to the world. So we have found that the process of getting to know others and to share talk and experiences with them draws us out into deeper awareness of life and indeed of God. This drawing out continues in our relationship with God. For most of us this is experienced in a growing relationship with Jesus. As we take note of him in the gospel we find his words make demands 'Go and do thou likewise', 'Give to them that ask.' But Jesus does not only say challenging things, he works them out in practice with all the difficulties they involve. He suffers and dies; it is not only his words which compel attention, but even more his life and death. This could be alarming, as we sometimes find the expertise and efficiency of the able person somewhat frightening. However, Jesus does it all so humbly, with such concern for others, not only in their physical weakness but also in their moral and personal failure; the paralysed man saw the point when Jesus said to him 'Son, thy sin be forgiven' (Mark 2.5).

As any counsellor knows it is genuine concern and acceptance, indeed love, which turns and draws men and women out of themselves, and begins to change them, bringing them to a point where they can accept forgiveness and change. It may dawn on us gradually that God is interested in us and in fact gives a good deal of care, and may be wanting from us to turn out from self to love for others and for him. It may very well be through moments of wonder at the splendour of nature, for instance that we see something of our own littleness and pettiness. We may get some sense of the generosity of God in life and of others around us, and in contrast see something of our own meanness. Thanking is a way of becoming aware; very simply we are reminded of how good other people are to us, and so reminded how difficult we often are in return. We may go on to see how things have gone well for us, and to be thankful for what we have been able to do. At the same time, we can often see how things might have been better if we had behaved differently.

The common response at this point is regret, but regret can be very negative. It can decay, in fact, into remorse if we turn in on ourselves, and become sorry for ourselves. We need to turn outwards, and see that these things matter, not so much to us but to others, and to God. We need to be sorry not so much for ourselves but for others and to others, to be sorry for God and to God.

In the story of the prodigal son Jesus makes it very clear to us that God is waiting for us and coming to meet us with his forgiveness. Humility and honesty can open us to understand and receive his forgiveness, and this can give us immense help and assurance to be honest with other people. Very often this assurance will enable us to discover that other people are much more ready to move towards us and accept and forgive us. On the other hand, sometimes we find they are not, because they are just as mixed up as we are. This shouldn't surprise us. The forgiveness of God can help us here too. We can realize that God is very patient with us, so we need to be patient with other people. At the same time God is very hopeful with us, and we ought to be hopeful with other people. He certainly expects us to be forgiving of others – Jesus taught us to pray 'Forgive us our trespasses, as we forgive them that trespass against us.'

Forgiveness isn't a negative thing, though we sometimes reduce it to that. God doesn't; he not only accepts, but he renews and changes us step by step. 'Can he really change us?', we wonder, when we fall into the same old trap. 'Isn't this the trouble with the same old human nature?' The New Testament writers offer the good news that God can and does change human life; they point us to the life and death of Jesus, accepting life, in all its ramifications, its muddles and failures, its disaster and death in trust and being answered. You can see how contact with the risen Jesus changed the shattered disciples into men of real strength, so that they not only had the physical courage to stand up and be counted, and often killed, but also the moral strength to commend an attitude to life so vigorously that it could eventually spread across the world. There must have been some very real depth in the change there.

This change is epitomised in the conversion or turning, of Saul of Tarsus into Paul the apostle and writer. Paul started as a confident Pharisee, but on his own admission, a proud and covetous one. He found himself confronted with the forgiving way of Jesus which he fought to suppress. To his surprise he found that in dependence on the forgiveness and generosity of

God he was able to teach others the meaning of love and co-operation. It is worth trying to understand Paul's letters on the subject, particularly that to the Romans, with the help of new translations of the New Testament. You can see his deep understanding of the way we act against the good we see, 'The good which I want to do I fail to do. What I do is the wrong, which is against my will.' He found out of his own experience that rules, as in the Jewish Law, were powerless to deal with the deep attitudes and desires. These can only be changed by the possibility of outside help, which to his surprise he found was given in the death and resurrection of Jesus of Nazareth, whom he had completely misjudged. He found that in co-operation with Jesus he could have a changed and humble assurance in God, to replace an anxious self-assurance.

It is interesting that Paul talks about faith mostly in connection with what he described as being justified by faith. There is, of course, a whole background in the Old Testament about the justification or vindication of God. However, you can see something of what Paul means by this quite simply if you think of the number of times in a day we say or do something to justify ourselves, or silently justify ourselves to ourselves. Very often we know this is a false process; we could, indeed, save a lot of moral and mental energy, if we could drop this attempt to justify ourselves, and accept the fact that we can be accepted by other people, by life, by God.

Caseworkers have written copiously about the need to be accepted, and the further need to accept that we are accepted. Anyone who helps other people in personal trouble knows that they begin by helping the person to face the facts and to see themselves for what they are; they then need to go on to help that person to see that they can be accepted and used as they are and can go on from this point stage by stage. This normally requires some support in the process; it asks big questions – 'Is this all really possible?' This may be the spoken, or the unspoken question of the person being helped. It may be the nagging question of the helper and supporter, who becomes very conscious of his or her own need to be supported, and, indeed, justified.

Jesus in his words and his actions, and Paul in his experiences and his writings, spell out the answer of assurance, but certainly both make the point that you must try it and see. We must try turning and accepting forgiveness. There may be vivid moments when we are stopped in our tracks and come to our senses, and these can be moments when we find ourselves praying honestly and humbly, and looking for forgiveness. For much of our lives, however, we tend not to stop, but to limp on, and so it is the end of the day when we have our best chance; as we thought, we may very well be helped to see things clearly by starting with some thanksgiving, and then go on to look honestly at our failure. We may remind ourselves of Christ's standard, and of his help and forgiveness, from the gospel. We shall certainly want to look forward to using his forgiveness, and we may very well pick up the thought again in the morning, to look forward to the coming day, to trust his power to help us further.

We may see more of this power if we stop to look back over a week at its end. Over a longer period we see more of the subtlety of the goodness and help we have received and can thank God for it; so, too, we can see more of our responsibilities and of our failures. We get a chance to look into our deeper attitudes, and from this we can look forward to the new week and claim the forgiveness and help of Christ. We can claim it confidently, in the knowledge that Jesus rose on the first day of the week. It is not for nothing that Christians have kept this first day of the week for worship; it is not for nothing that Jesus gave them the way of sharing his dying and rising in the act of communion. It makes a natural focus and basis for our turning and changing over the weeks.

Explore the way of turning, explore accepting forgiveness, of trusting God's justification and acceptance of us, which is for Paul the basic experience of faith. Some are surprised by this, having thought that faith was an intellectual or mystical exercise. Yet the process presented both in Paul's letters, and in Jesus' dealing with men and women, directs us to the practical tasks of coming to ourselves, to our senses, and accepting the help of God to come out of ourselves in trust towards others and towards him. Jesus is very aware that some will react from this, and some will try to shrug it off, but this is a central task of life, a main way into prayer and God.

9 *Engaging*

Doors and gates open ways to new fields and to new situations. They occur at stages on the way, from one property to another. They require a little attention to a latch, and sometimes not a little resolution to make up one's mind that it is safe to go through to the new territory. Some have difficulties about decisions; this is not surprising, and no cause for alarm. Of course it is a handicap if people spend a long time dithering, and they can become neurotic about it. On the other hand, others, who like making decisions, may make things more difficult for others by concentrating too much attention on this matter.

We pass through various stages of life as we grow up. In the earlier stages the gates are natural enough, as we master walking and talking, but each takes us into a vastly wider world. The further stages of education often have formidable doors, some actually labelled Infants, Juniors, Seniors. These lead to positive hurdles in public examinations, entrance and other qualifications. These are not the end, indeed only the beginning, of adult life, with its further stages of engagement, marriage and family, moves in work and house, and finally retirement. Each of these asks for some decisive response, some engagement of ourselves; it may be sudden, or more likely more gradual. There will be involvement with a particular person in marriage or work with whom you must come to terms; in return we shall find we are given a new view and opportunity.

The Bible shows us God meeting his children in particular ways, at particular times, through particular people. He chose Abraham and the family of Jacob, and then, as Paul put it to the Galatians 4.4: 'When the fullness of time came God sent forth his Son, born of a woman.' Jesus chose twelve men and did particular things with them. In particular he gave them his acts of baptism and the breaking of bread. So God has continued to work through particular times, calling out particular people in them, in Dark and Middle Ages, in the Reformation and Revivals. But God's particularity isn't confined to notable people; he offers himself to each one of us in a particular relationship of prayer and sacrament, and in what has been wisely called 'the sacrament of the present moment' – each passing moment in all its new possibility.

The moments of life, special or ordinary, need to be grasped. We need not screw ourselves into great agonies of decision, but we do need to engage life. God in fact helps us to do this by the ways in which he offers himself to us in particular ways: responding to these enables us to respond to life. The simple looking at the day which we have discussed, looking to see how much there is to thank God for and to see where we must turn and change, will certainly help us to engage life, to get into more genuine contact with it. The thinking we do, either starting from life and seeing the critique that God brings to it, or working the other way round, will often lead us to particular resolutions. The stirring to share our care for others with God in prayer does mean that we will actually do at least this for others. It will soon stir our consciences to do more in specific action.

Praying can indeed get us going to commit ourselves to life. It may be a help on the way to doing this to commit ourselves to relate each day to God. This may seem a big undertaking to some, a big step to take; others will find that the lines we have followed so far begin to converge, and there is an obvious door to go through. It does lead on to a new stage, where we can begin to look further about relating life to God and we can look into that later.

This may seem to some to be rushing on too fast and too far. Are we convinced that the door leads anywhere? Isn't this really too big an act of faith, and isn't faith a big question we have not yet reached? But we have already thought that issues of faith are being raised all along. They are raised in our first wondering about life, about its further dimensions; they are raised again as we see how much we have been given in life, and how much there is that we come to take for granted and to trust. It is raised again as we find ourselves caring about life for ourselves and for others, and yearning about it, and looking for help. Here our belief that life should and can be different is a simple but deep testimony of our trust in the goodness of life and of God. When we turn to see that we, too, ought to be different, we may find ourselves saying we believe we could be, and then are half way to learning Paul's lesson of justification by faith.

The point is being made to us quietly but repeatedly; the lines converge. We do, in fact, stand at the gate of faith and are probably through it without realizing it. We don't stand alone. If we use the consciousness we've gained on the way of Jesus of Nazareth, and the possibility of relationship with him, we can know that we are not alone, we can know that God has come to meet us in him and to take us by the hand. It is not too difficult to take this hand and engage the Christian faith. We can commit ourselves to it and say with Paul 'God was in Christ reconciling the world to himself' (II Cor. 5.19) and 'The love of God is shed abroad in our hearts by the Spirit he has given us' (Rom. 5.5).

It is a help to be able to borrow words, and see the practical way in which others have found faith and relationship to God in prayer. We find here the use of prayers, hymns, scriptures. As we have thought, there is much to be gained from looking for God with others. We may very well look to find God through engaging in the church's worship. We can only find its effectiveness by trying and seeing, but trying means really trying to enter into it, to find out something about it, so that we can participate with some understanding.

It is worth understanding that Christian worship centres in the specific offers of Christ to relate himself to us in his dying and rising. He offers an individual beginning to this relationship in the clean start of baptism, and the confirmation of the laying on of hands of the Bishop, the personal representative of the continuing Christian community; in these acts we share in the dying and rising of Christ, and the gift of the Spirit. It is natural that Christians have come to want to begin this relationship at the first stages of human life, and that many parts of the church have spread this act out over the stages of growth by leaving confirmation to one or other of the stages of childhood – seven, eleven, or sixteen, in different churches. So baptism and confirmation give us natural ways to engage Christ, as we meet different stages of life, and move on to new fields.

Then Christ gives us the completed gift of himself, dying and rising, in communion. Christians were quick to pick up the reminder of the resurrection on the first day of the week, and use this gift for the beginning of each new week. Here is a handle to open the door to a new stage, a clear reminder that we do not pass the new stage alone, but in communion with him. There is much more to discuss about communion and we must have a look at this later, but for the present we need to be clear that communion is the place to engage life with God. It is not a distant stage of the way for an elite; it is certainly a way in to find God and to find prayer It can help us quite simply to realize that relationship with God is nothing less than communion with him. Further communion gives us a way of sharing the dying and rising of Christ; it offers a pledge of the possibility of change in ourselves and in the world.

'All this sounds very grand, but I don't want to get involved with the church or with others.' It is strange that people react in this way, when they also tend to judge Christ by his followers. If we begin to want to be committed to him, we ought to join the other followers. If we feel they need a good deal of change, we must be prepared to take a share in effecting that change. After all, we admire Jesus greatly because he became involved in human life; he did something about the religious life of his time, he worked with his half-hearted disciples; you might add, he is prepared to be involved with us today, in our double-mindedness. So we may try to respond, and be prepared to engage with him and his followers, hesitant though we may be, but trusting he may do something with us, as he did with those disciples.

'But I don't want to be committed', is a great cry today in all sorts of fields. Strange to say, it's accompanied by another cry of wanting to be secure. So people rush into early marriages, and then say they didn't really mean to commit themselves for life. They clearly ought to have thought more about engagement in more ways than one. So we can think about engagement to God in more ways than one! There is a sense in which God is content for us to move from point to point, from stage to stage. We may move to the stage of trying to commit ourselves to daily prayer. We may move further, to recognizing a commitment to Christ; we can try out worship in the church, we can explore confirmation and communion. We may approach the stages hesitantly, but we shall often find God more easily and more quickly than we think; for the engagement is not one-sided; he loves us and engages us.

10 *Exploring – The Way On*

Marriages are not made in a moment. Most of us first need a fair period of courting and wooing, and then a further period of engagement before the actual wedding. Wedding services don't make marriages, however; they only begin them. So couples discover, some to their cost and others to their joy; a marriage goes on being fashioned day by day and grows according to its experience. For many this is the simple growth in learning another person's point of view, of discovering new ways of doing things, becoming more tolerant and more sensitive and imaginative. For others, alas, this is a series of rude shocks and disillusionments; 'it's not what I got married for', is a remark which betrays the failure to appreciate the need to work to make a marriage. For those who are prepared to work and to explore new ways, even from difficult beginnings, there are pleasant surprises ahead. As the experience of love grows deeper, they may find there is a real ecstasy in being drawn out of ourselves.

It is much the same with prayer. The relationship with God isn't made all at once. We don't buy it ready made, off the peg. It has to be made stage by stage with day to day business of living. For many there will be difficult periods when God seems hard to understand; 'What do I get out of it?' is the anguished cry, echoing that of the disappointed marriage partner. But this complaint also reveals a failure to appreciate and to respond to the need to work to make a relationship of prayer. Here, too, there is a need to explore even from difficult beginnings. There is a possibility of discovering gradually a new point of view; there are new ways of doing things in prayer to explore. We find that loving God can become a real experience and one that has deeper and deeper meaning. Here, too, there is a genuine ecstasy to be found of being drawn out of ourselves.

It's dangerous to press analogies too far. The marriage analogy may give a misleading suggestion, that there is a definite division between the courting period and the growing part of prayer, between the way in and the way on. The long experience of praying people gives a reassuring answer at this point to those who feel that they can never cross this dividing line. Most of us who pray would be the first to admit we do so very patchily; it may be in fits and starts, or more likely that the starts and parts of prayer are very thin and easily distracted. Most will say that we are still in the process of finding prayer; and the patches may need to be filled in, or rather filled out.

At the same time, some may be feeling that the old patches are all too worn, and familiar; they have gone over the ground time and again. These people need very much to explore new ground, to reach out further, above all to explore the possibility of really looking at God and being drawn to love him deeply. There is always room to grow in prayer.

Yet those who have hardly begun to pray need not feel confined to the ways of looking we have suggested. They can take encouragement from those who do pray, but pray patchily, and realize the patches of possibilities which they have begun to see may gradually piece together for them also. Yet there is still more to be found by reaching out further. They too will find that they do in fact already have some experience of looking at God, though they hardly recognize it; they have some moments of wanting to love, and to love deeply, though they may hardly like to admit it. It is a pity to neglect these moments and experience; we need to explore them. Even the most hesitant, who wonder whether there are any ways in for them, would do well to look further and to begin to explore the way on.

Some, both believers and unbelievers, will want to press the marriage analogy further, and say 'Don't you really have to commit yourself at some definite point, in prayer as well as in marriage?' There is an obvious attraction in this view, and for some the attraction is compelling. It is the very attraction of this argument that helps some to find a commitment to God. Some may come to such a definite point by the effect of some particular experience of God, often through some particular person. This can be an obvious blessing, but this sudden way of commitment is not for everyone, and probably not the way for the majority.

For most of us commitment to God, making a relationship with him, is a matter of building up gradually. It is rather like sinking piles in a river to build a bridge; for a long time nothing appears above the surface, but gradually the piers rise, and are able to carry a bridge. The bridge rests on the piles below the surface. So too we gradually accumulate experience of finding God, and this in the end is able to bear the weight of a relationship with him which can carry the traffic of relating daily life to him in prayer. Much more depends on the hidden first experiences than we realize, but they need completion by the steady building on of fresh layers. So most of us need to go on from the first reaching after God, to explore further ways of relating to him, so that we gradually accumulate a sufficient experience to be at home with God. It will not be surprising if the previous discussion of ways in has left some readers interested but only half convinced that there is something in all this. They will need to go on; although not every further explanation will appeal to them, they may be able to accumulate enough to find the relationship with God, to find themselves at home with him.

In this process of accumulation we gradually become conscious that it has been going on a long time, at least from God's side. We can look back and see various things in life which have helped us, and others which have hindered; we become conscious of God's interest and care for us through all sorts of ups and downs. Even those who have some compelling experience and come to sudden commitment are generally very aware that the initiative has come from God, and that in a sense he has been there all the time. Even Paul, with his vivid confrontation on the road to Damascus, could speak of God separating him from his mother's womb (Gal. 1.15).

So we might say this sort of marriage goes right back to the beginning, and that all our life is a working out of this close relationship. It comes from the initiative of God, from his being there in the first place, which is called his prevenience. For many Christians this has been expressed in the specific act of infant baptism. Whichever way we express it, there is a sense in which we can rely on the fact that God's love for us is there first 'We love because he loved us first', as John's first epistle puts it (I John 4.19). We spend our whole life waking up to this fact; it's up to us to explore it and respond to it fully.

The content of this relationship with God is, of course, infinite. We shall not unpack it fully this side of death. But there is a good deal to explore in the span of life available to us. So we need, in a sense, an infinite ambition in prayer; this is not a selfish ambition for it must be an ambition to come out of ourselves more. This isn't to say that the aim is to reach a state of abstraction, either of pure thought or absolute blank, as some eastern religions suggest. The medieval Christian mystic's description of it as self-naughting may mislead some, but this description has a great point. But this point is subsidiary to the end of love, of a personal love of a personal living God which implies a full love for his children. Love God and love your neighbour, Jesus said to the ambitious young Jew, and there is ambition enough here to take us through death, and to enable us to see dying as part of living, of giving of ourselves.

Psychiatrists re-echo those words of John's epistle, 'we love because he loved us first'; our ability to love grows out of our experience of being loved. It grows most easily if we are fortunate enough to be blessed with loving parents and others around us, but it can still grow, even with those who have missed out on this blessing, as they come to discover God's direct care for them. It may be through the very difficulties of life that people discover the thread, sometimes very thin, of care which has come to them through all sorts of unsuspected hands. This care, even the fragmentary nature of it may lead them to appreciate the care and interest of God which has put it together into their life. They may begin to realize God is really interested in them. We all need to discover this: we need to put together our experience of care, easy or difficult, as it may have come to us. As we do this we shall realize that there is much more to explore in this interest and relationship which God has in and with us.

All our love is our response to our being held by the love of God in one way or another. So a beginning of our growing in communication with God in prayer is growing in our sense of belonging, in realizing and recalling this fact. This is the truth underneath the traditional word of recollection for the initial act of concentration in prayer. But it is much more than a negative act, abstracting ourselves from other attentions, and attending to him, important though that is; it is a positive attention to the wonderful love with which he embraces us. So we must attend to him, and to our belonging to him further.

11 *Belonging*

Our early experience of relationships colours our future life deeply, either with light or shade. Yet even the shade sometimes throws up things in relief. Though good relationships in families are a great advantage, those who have lacked them may come to look for them in later life all the more. If they find wise and sympathetic help which they can use positively, they will come to value relationships all the more, and can be amongst those who help others most deeply. It is all the more so with God, who never stands aloof, but in all sorts of ways, by this offer and that, is waiting to show the person that he too belongs.

God's offer may be made through particular human friends, but it may be given through some corporate effort or institution, it may be given through the corporate institutional life of the church – providing the door stands open, services are at regular times, and clergy on tap. It may be the pages of the New Testament which give the first pointers towards the possibility of relationship with God. In all sorts of ways God is there waiting, he is there before we are, waiting to show us that he accepts us, and that we belong to him. For many, as we have thought, this prevenience and this belongingness is very simply represented in infant baptism. There, before we can respond, God accepts us, claiming us as his children, in union with Christ in the Spirit. Of course, Christians who practise infant baptism believe it only makes sense and only works through the corporate life of the church and family. In any case the corporate life around the child will affect him or her for good or ill; why should we not claim it for good, with the New Testament promise of baptism in the name of Christ and the relationship of the Spirit? Baptism gives a person a definite link to which to go back and gives a focus for the sense of belonging. Of course a person also needs to go on to understand it and to develop it.

The link is not based on the isolated act of baptism. Christian baptism is very clearly based on the death and resurrection of Jesus, and early on Christians became convinced that this in itself was no isolated act. They soon came to see that Jesus had been facing not only the opposition of the leaders of his nation but the opposition of all men and women to the rule of God. They saw that his complete self-giving to God and man, and his complete trust in God were an answer to all this, and his resurrection was the vindication of it. They discovered, moreover, that they could continue to have relationship with the living Jesus after he had left them by the activity within themselves of the Holy Spirit.

So the New Testament thinks of Jesus' death and resurrection redeeming the world. Men and women need to accept this, and to act upon it in relationship with him; it is there for the taking. We can be, or rather we are, redeemed. We are accepted. We can be, or rather we are, related. We can and do belong to Our Father. The alternative of 'can' and 'do' is part of his love, which will not force itself upon us. It is much closer to us than we often realize. We can help ourselves to realize it if we exercise that freedom he has given us to make a move on our part, or take hold of that relationship with God, to express our belonging, to recall, to recollect it.

The recollection and expression of this relationship is simpler than we often think. Even the difficulty of concentration is much less than we fear, if we can realize God is no inactive spectator. Too often we picture the effort to start praying as one of catching God, as it were running after him with a lasso of prayer, to catch, or we see prayer as sitting very still and setting an elaborate trap to catch God. These are unflattering cartoons, but the techniques of approaching God are often unflattering to him. The great Christian tradition of prayer as shown in Paul's and

John's letters is that God finds us, and we wake up to him. More particularly it is based on the fact that men and women have found God at work in human life in Jesus. Jesus faced life at its worst, right to death, in love and trust, and was raised, and through the Spirit he shares his risen life with us. By his ascension we know that Jesus is completely one with Our Father, still sharing our human life, and through the Spirit we can share that communion with God with him.

This is why our prayers in church often end 'through Jesus Christ Our Lord'. Sometimes this continues with the fuller form 'Who liveth and reigneth with thee in the unity of the Holy Spirit.' These are not just archaic formulae; they are working formulae, and they tell you how Christian prayer works. This is not by the lasso or the trap, but if you like, by the pulley, of Christ's life and death and resurrection and the outreach of the Spirit. It is better to put it in a human picture, that Christ takes us by the hand of the Spirit to lead us to our Father.

These suggest some other simple thoughts and pictures. All this means that we never pray alone; the letter to the Hebrews says 'He ever lives to make intercession for us' (Heb. 7.25). Christ is always praying with us. We can be sure, too, that other Christians are praying, some actually at the same time as us, even if not in our family or round the corner, somewhere across the world. We are more closely linked to them than we think, for Paul gives us the vivid picture that through the work of the Spirit we are used as limbs of Christ's body on earth, and therefore we are all interdependent. So you might draw another crude picture, and say that prayer is always a matter of travelling by bus, an omnibus, for all. This corrects another false picture of prayer which might be described as travelling by private taxi at considerable expense. Any experience we have had of trying to think and pray with other people in groups or in the common prayer of the church, will have taught us how much we gain from the expression of this interdependence.

These crude pictures may clear away a few misconceptions. We would do better to return to the personal language of the

New Testament, to give us a start in prayer. One obvious help is actually the conclusion of one of Paul's letters to the Corinthians, the familiar formula of 'the grace of our Lord Jesus Christ, and the love of God, and the fellowship of the Holy Spirit'. From this Christian tradition went on to derive the simple invocation 'in the name of the Father, and of the Son and of the Holy Spirit', which has often been accompanied or symbolized by the making of the sign of the cross, taking us back to the basic redemption of the world by Christ's death and resurrection.

For others, reality of prayer through the Spirit with Christ to our Father is best summed up in the prayer which Christ taught us, Our Father. We have already thought of the importance of Jesus' teaching his disciples to speak to God as Father. This can be a great thought to start us off in our prayer, and to which to return in our prayer, though the actual text takes us into the midst of Jesus' teaching about the kingdom or rule of God, and the crisis he saw ahead. The full understanding of this leads to the deepest theological considerations, but its width is such that it can carry many lesser thoughts. The Lord's Prayer may provide a whole framework for some; it is possible to use it phrase by phrase, slowly, filling it out with our own thoughts. This is splendidly done in George Appleton's book of prayers *In his Name*.

For most of us, the value of the great phrases, such as the Grace, or the Invocation, or the Lord's Prayer, is to give us a simple act by which we can enter consciously into prayer. They each offer an act by which we can recollect quickly what we are doing and can pick up that deep relationship by which God holds us. These acts can be of use not only at the beginning, but at moments through our prayers when our attention wanders, or can remind us that we do not pray alone. In our patchy prayer they help us to persevere, knowing the Spirit fills our prayers, and links us with others in Christ.

Our sense of relationship to God will give us the confidence to think more deeply about the relationship of all our life to God. Prayer is the place to start doing this – by bringing into conscious review events of the day. Newspaper articles and sermons often plead for more every day religion, not for Sundays only, but for Monday to Saturday too. Though everybody agrees with the need to integrate religion and life, it's often difficult to do it in the heat of the moment. The link needs to be made, and made by daily prayer. But this isn't to be the dour struggle to which it has so often been reduced. It is not a matter of a daily expedition to lasso God, or the daily expense of a taxi. It is a matter of waking up to life, which we have to do every morning, and waking up to the fact that we and life belong to our Father; we need to pick ourselves up, and pick up the relationship with God.

12 *Relating*

Relating life to God is a good test of reality of prayer. Prayer, if it means anything cannot be just a resting in God's company. The God of the Bible is certainly the living God, who creates and sustains the world, so he will want us to be relating our life and the world to him in prayer. The knowledge that we belong to him, and that we pray with Christ to Our Father should rescue us from the painful situation of just saying prayers because we feel we ought to. We may feel we ought to do this in quite a refined way, going through the different parts of prayer, thanksgiving, penitence, intercession for instance, but if they're no more than this, they're rather like those parts of a construction kit for a model aircraft which never get off the ground.

In fact we need to rescue prayer from all mechanical pictures, and go by the way of looking at the relationship with our Father and what it entails. It will entail the different parts of prayer, but they will make sense, and integrate life, in this relationship with its creator. The simple thought of praying with Christ to our Father is enough to start us on this course. On the course we shall have to look well at the coasts of life and the tides of its seas, but we shall also need to consult chart and compass, and get to know the mind of the master. We shall need to give further attention to that prayer of thinking of which we thought earlier, the prayer of getting to know God in Christ, and his will, often with the help of the gospels. We shall have to think about attending to God, and knowing and loving him more. But first let us look at life from the starting point of relationship with God.

There is always a struggle in the minds of men and women as to whether they look first at the goodness of the world or at its defects. Caseworkers will tell you this initial response, too, is a reflection of childhood experience. We begin our prayers from the base of our belonging to our Father, it would seem natural to go on to see the goodness of the world, and to rejoice in it in thanksgiving and praise. It is interesting to reflect how at various points in the church's history men and women, great men and women at that, have started by looking at the wrong in the world, and human failure. This is reflected in our 1662 Prayer Book, which begins morning and evening prayer with the penitential introduction which was prefixed under Puritan influence in 1552 to the more traditional opening of 'O Lord, open thou our lips: and our mouths shall show forth thy praise.' For many reasons the earlier tradition was healthier.

There is much to be said for going from the first recollection of prayer straight into thanksgiving. As we thought earlier, thanksgiving is one of the simplest ways to enter into prayer. It is an obvious way to begin to relate the days to God, to look back and see what has happened to us and to see what we have been enabled to do. In this way we can begin to see further into our daily life, and to see something of its significance for God and ourselves. From this we can usefully extend thanksgiving to the morning. In the evening we notice the particular things of the past day, but there is much that we simply take for granted. All this is still there in the morning; 'thank God it is', you might very well say, so take the trouble to thank him in the morning for some regular part of life. It is wise to concentrate on one part on one morning, so that we can give proper attention to it, and not just a passing nod.

A particular point of thanksgiving is to help us to stop and think and pray in the rush of the morning. It is not very difficult to choose six aspects of life to look at on the mornings of the week, leaving Sunday to the gathering up of the past week. Some may quite happily find ample and fresh thoughts for thankfulness each morning without any further prompting, but many would be helped to have a simple list in the mind, or it may be on paper, for the days of the week. Such a list might include such areas as family and friends, our own health and abilities, our work, society around us, the world at large, and the church of God. We may take this further, and jot down some points under each heading from different stages or parts of life and different contacts. Some may like to borrow phrases of classical prayers, psalms, hymns, to sum up and express their thanks. Lancelot Andrewes' *Preces Privatae* gives us a wonderful sample from the sixteenth century of just such a collection of personal thanksgivings for each day.

It is through this opening up of thanksgiving that most find their easiest way to pass on from thanking God for his gifts to praising him for himself. Some hardy spirits will plunge straight into this, and into the further depths of adoration. They are in many ways fortunate, but they too, need to be thankful. Most of us have to wade down from the shallow end of thanksgiving. We may find ourselves swimming happily in a pool of praise, at any rate from time to time. Most of us, in fact, will need to plumb greater depths through the prayer of thinking and looking before we dive into adoration.

If it is right for most to look first at the goodness of God, we probably ought not to delay the facing of failure longer in our prayers, at least in the evening. Of course, there may be times when this has to be attended to first. This may be true of any part of prayer; we certainly need to be flexible in our prayer. We have already had to realize that we are made in very different ways, and no one runs exactly to type or runs the same all the time; we must be prepared to vary.

This will be particularly true of penitence. We may want to express penitence very definitely on some days, but not want to do very much on others. We must not force it, yet we must keep in mind the distinction between want and need. We need to carry in our minds an awareness of Christ's love, and the response it asks. Putting thanksgiving first will help us to do this; as we see the good there has been in the day, we see at the same time where things haven't been so good, through our failure. We can think of the generosity of Christ, even to the point of death, and we can remember the gift of the Spirit and the fruit that he is trying to grow in us, love, joy, peace and so on. This may begin to make us conscious that we often miss the mark, which is one of the root meanings of the word for sin in the common Greek of the New Testament.

All this may come to mind quite briefly on some evenings; on others some particular matter will hold us longer. We need to recall the basic fact of God's acceptance of us, and the power of Christ's forgiveness. We may well turn this to the thought of resolution for the next morning, when we should be looking forward. It may be possible to form some small particular resolve, and pick it up the next morning, perhaps attaching it to some particular act in the day, or it may be a matter of looking to a particular attitude. Both penitence and resolution are points of prayer where we can most easily see the need for looking over the longer span of the week or the seasons, the points at which we see the need of renewal, to which we must return.

The rhythm of the days can help us with what is for many the most obvious point at which we relate the day to God, the prayer of caring or intercession. Once we have seen the possibility of sharing this care with God in Christ, the claim of intercession becomes pressing. Television may help us to visualize the need, but may serve to make it almost overwhelming. We can break it down over the days. We may well follow the pattern we considered for thanksgiving, praying for the needs we have encountered during the day in the evening, and then in the morning praying for different areas of life, under the same heads as our thanksgiving. For others it will be simple to do things the other way round, in the morning to pray for those they are to meet in the coming day and in the evening to pray for the different areas of life round the week. Either may seem too ambitious a programme for some; they will find it all they can do to pray briefly in the morning, with a short thanksgiving and a looking forward to the day. Yet they might do well to spread their thoughts rather more in the evening, and to pray for their friends and concerns in turn.

There will, of course, be some people such as family and close colleagues, for whom we shall want to pray every day, and others for whom we must pray on this particular day; it may be a day of particular sickness or particular undertakings or a celebration. Beyond this we need some simple plan; we often discover this need by default. We say we will pray for someone and then we discover we have never really done so after the first day; it was too much to remember. The simplest way is to have some lists, either in the mind or on paper. We need to group them in some sort of arrangement by their concerns or different parts of life. The list may be prayed through quite briefly, with a quick thought for each; at times we may take in one part of the list at a glance in order to give particular attention to another part – this will be quite fair. It's a help for most people to write the list down and to keep the list by the bedside. For those whose work involves direct contact with several people, such as clergy, social workers, doctors or teachers, a list in a diary may be a help both in prayer and in daily business. Incidentally, praying regularly about a person is a great help towards remembering their names and really getting to know that person.

This last is a practical example of the way in which the relating of life to God is made possible by the daily round of prayer. There is plenty of evidence of the value of the daily round, indeed a twice-daily round. This rhythm is in itself a help, a help to see life whole. Different times of day will suit different people; for some first thing in the morning and last thing at night is quite the easiest, for others the morning time may be after seeing children off to school, and for others the evening will be best at its beginning, when they've got home from work. However much one time in the day may be best for the greater part of prayer, we need the quick act at the other end of the day. These times are insertions of thin ends of wedges into the day and are themselves a significant act of getting further into prayer. They begin to open up the whole day and the whole of life to God.

We should certainly be on the look out for other opportunities to open up the cracks of the day. It may be the quick arrow prayer as we face some task or meeting, or begin some piece of work. It may be the opportunity to pray in a quiet church at some stage of the day, or it may be simply in a time of waiting for a train or bus. All these are very right and natural expressions of our relation with our Father and our relating life to him. They are much more likely to happen and to be meaningful if they spring out of a relationship built up on regular contacts. They are of course available to all, and some will say it is their only form of praying. They may be for a time, but in that time they will in fact be drawing on past times of relationship; and these times will in fact be an invitation to pick up the threads of that relationship and to weave the regular round of the day into it.

13 *Looking*

Relating life to God means looking not only at life but also at God. It asks us not just to give him a prefunctory nod or occasional attention, but to look at him with some frequency and regularity, so that we begin to get to know him in depth. For most of us, as we have thought, the place to begin is in the gospels, where men came to realize that in the human life of Jesus of Nazareth they had seen God at work. There are certainly other ways in which to look at God. Jesus himself pointed men and women to look at the world around them, and we can well follow his hints, and so go on to have our own ideas about ways for looking at God. Yet we shall find it wise to bring these back to compare with the hints of Jesus. In a very real way Jesus provides the norm for looking at God.

In another sense he does also, for in the life and death of Jesus men came to see that God was involved in human life, right up to the neck, you might say. They learned once and for all that God does not stand aloof from the world he has created. He does his work within the world of time and change, of pain and suffering. Men learned this deeply enough to sustain it against a heavy tide of Greek thought which conceived God as quite apart from time and change, and pain and suffering. This was a difficult point to sustain; at times the church only sustained it by holding on to the real humanity of Christ, while having an excessively transcendent view of the Father. Nowadays there is a greater readiness to admit that the revelation in Christ shows us that it is the nature of God to be involved. Yes, he is transcendent, mysterious, and the almighty creator, but that does not mean that he stands apart or is remote from suffering.

This is not just an academic point; it affects our relationship to God. Those who look for a God apart remove themselves from worldly involvement; certainly some Christian mystics have done this at various times, but they have always found the words of Christ challenging them to human concerns. Looking at God incarnate, involved, always calls us to some involvement. As we get to know God in Christ we cannot remain indifferent. If we admire him we must agree with him, and want to follow him. As the old prayer of St Richard of Chichester puts it,

> May I know thee more clearly,
> Love thee more dearly,
> Follow thee more nearly.

The prayer of looking at God in Christ and getting to know him is not an academic option for the intellectual, it is the common-sense way of discovering and deepening the friendship of God. True friendship implies agreement in doing things together.

There is good traditional advice that the way to begin to deepen relationship with God in prayer is by thinking or meditating about the gospels. Take a short passage from the gospels, one paragraph, maybe a parable or action of Jesus, or a group of short sayings. Try to see what Jesus was getting at in it; quite often the early church, in telling the story, has made some points stand out in a sort of punchline 'The first shall be last, and the last first', 'The Son of Man has power on earth to forgive sins'. Think why they thought this worth preserving, and what it says for us today, then bring it down to what Jesus may be saying to you through this, at this particular point. Think what you can do about it; it may be some small act, but better a small one that really will happen in the next twenty-four hours than a big one which may never come your way. Increasingly, you may find that the response cannot be isolated in one act, but is much more a matter of attitude. It is useful to mark that attitude clearly and to check it later. In many ways it is good to do this thinking or meditating about the gospels in the morning, so that we can work out our response during the day. This may, however, be tricky to organize, and for many the possibilities come in the evening. In that case it's worth carrying a thought of a resolution or attitude over to the next morning, to work out in that day.

It isn't very difficult to see that one test of the reality of prayer is the difference it makes to our behaviour and the quality of our life; 'by their fruits you shall know them' is certainly the view of our neighbours, as well as of the gospel. So this process of deepening prayer in looking at Jesus in the gospel, must be a process of changing our behaviour. Tradition has called this way of prayer the purgative way, emphasizing this process of changing or cleansing our lives. The word has unfortunate associations today both in the medicinal and political directions. Yet the point is fair enough; we need a time of getting down to the business of sorting out what living in friendship with God in Christ really means for us. It needs spelling out, and the gospels are a great help for us in doing this. We skip coming to grips with the content of the gospels at our peril.

As we have thought, the outcome of such prayer may come to be expressed not so much in an act as in an attitude. Attitudes go deep, and are only gradually changed; we have to see new things to change them, and find new affections. Prayer becomes not so much a matter of straight resolution but much more of long term yearning. At the same time our attention is turned from dwelling on what Jesus says to looking at him himself. We certainly do this through what he says and does, but want to go on to looking at him himself. We need to think not only of what we ought to do, but how we might possibly begin to do it with his help, and the need to trust and love him more.

We find it difficult to express this; we generally find the most possible way is in short repeated phrases, and often we are glad to borrow these from hymns and scripture. We may also use the simple phrases of human affection and yearning. This kind of prayer goes through dark and light phases, and we must think much more about them later, but it is certainly a way that is on the main track of prayer, and a time when we can know that we really are on the track. We begin to see and care more deeply, for Jesus' sake and not just our own. We begin to see a light ahead, and this part of the journey has been called 'the illuminative way'.

At times we begin to find that the sense of being on to something real is sufficiently clear and strong for us to be able to hold it in a concentration which is at the same time relaxed. We can look, and love, and trust. For some this looking arises quite simply from their looking at Christ in the gospels. Others, perhaps starting from the words of Jesus, are pushed to look into the mystery of the Godhead to the Father. Others still find themselves looking at God in the depth of their being, in the mystery of life, or in the precious gift of the present moment; this might be put as ways of contemplating God the Spirit.

Contemplating is a popular word today, but may be misleading. In the Christian tradition it does not mean standing apart; transcendent though God is, he does not separate himself from us and from our world, and we cannot stand apart, either from the world or from him. So looking at God is always looking in love, in commitment, in the deepest relationship which can only be described in terms of union; so this way of prayer is described as 'the unitive way'. This makes quite clear it is not a way of blankness and negation only, but is a very positive thinking and loving. But it also needs to be made clear that it is not just absorption; it has been better described in terms of spiritual marriage.

Though there is value of a rough and ready sorting out of different stages in prayer, this has had its danger, in tradition, of thinking that these stages are widely separated in time. We may find that we pass quite quickly from one way to another; we see points that make us yearn; sometimes we find that we want to stop, and look, and love. But then we may find ourselves high and dry, and need to go back and pick up fresh thoughts from the gospels, or perhaps from looking at life. And we need to look at ourselves more deeply. We need to feel free to move back and forward from one kind of prayer to another.

In that movement back and forwards, it is essential that we are prepared to take life with us, and also Christ's criticism and challenge within it. We need to return to the gospel and the purgative way at times. There is a danger that contemplation, either from an Eastern background or a superficial reading of Christian mysticism, may be acquired as a technique. Though this may go as far as teaching a need for relaxation and tolerance, it hardly ever comes to grips with the suffering of the world, or its moral failure, or with the need of renewal in our own failure. We must not overlook this last great need; it is indeed the important starting point.

So it's worth finding ways in which we can begin and return to looking at the challenge that God puts to us. The simplest starting points are the gospels; take one and work through it section by section. This gives us a fair chance to see what a particular evangelist is putting to us; it may be wise, therefore, to start with Mark, and to leave John till last. It may be a help to use one of the simple paperback commentaries such as the Torch, New English Bible, or Pelican series, or we may use something simple like the Bible Reading Fellowship notes. Yet we may find the gospels too formidable, or too familiar to read straight through, so we can take selections from them, such as parables, or actions of Jesus in dealing with people, or what he says about this or that part of life.

This may give us a way of using Paul's epistles, now made much more understandable in modern translations. From the later parts of many of Paul's letters, we can pick out some fairly straight talking on human life. From the earlier parts we can find sections which help us to understand Christ's work of redemption, and deepen our understanding of the response of repentance and faith. The Acts of the Apostles can give us some more scenes akin to the gospels, which will call out our admiration and challenge us to follow. For some this is also true of the Old Testament, but much greater selectivity is needed here. The Psalms have certainly been a storehouse of prayer for many; they are particularly helpful for the prayer of yearning and affection.

At the times when we come back to prayer or thinking we may

be helped by the later writing of others distilling their experience of Christianity, as a change from the direct New Testament. *The Imitation of Christ* is perhaps the most obvious example; it is indeed full of biblical quotation, but the arrangement makes its fresh appeal. From a later period, in a different vein, Bunyan's *Pilgrim's Progress* is in a biblical vein. There are, of course, scores of classical writers who have much to help us, more particularly with the prayer of yearning and looking. So François de Sales' *Introduction to the Devout Life* certainly has much helpful material on what is really the purgative way. There are many modern writers too; in different ways, Michael Quoist's *Prayers of Life* and *Christian Response*, and Dag Hammersköld's *Markings* have helped many different people to see God's challenge in life, and to set them doing their own looking at life.

A different but very real way of the prayer of looking may be to give a solid ten minutes or so, beginning by looking at some part of life going on around us and letting it come home to us. It may be some part of our own working life, it may be some part of the material world around us, or something in the natural world. This is, as we have thought, following the hints of Our Lord in the gospels, and there is certainly food for thought in them and challenges to us. We need to make sure that we do reach challenges, and don't just take the food for thought. Those hints of Jesus can act as a check.

In many ways we need to feel free to move. It's good to explore different ways of thinking and meditating, different uses of the gospel, different parts of the New Testament. It's good to look at different writers, and to try our own thing in different aspects of life. We may find ourselves taken on to the prayer of yearning, or to quiet looking and loving, and we shall find ourselves taken back and forward. And when we go back the variety of ways will be all the more useful. For one way or another, God is anxious to help us to grow into deep friendship with him, but it must be a real friendship, 'Can two walk together, except they be agreed?', as Amos said long ago (Amos 3.3). We must keep returning to God's challenge.

14 *Involving*

Friendship with Jesus Christ soon involves us in his activities, as we might expect from our experience of relationship with other people. You have only to think of some of his familiar parables, such as the Good Samaritan (Luke 10.29-37), with its pointed conclusion, 'Go, and do likewise', or think of the sharp contrast in the parable of the Sheep and the Goats (Matt. 25.31-46), 'Anything you did for one of my brothers here, however humble, you did for me' and 'Anything you did not do for one of these, however humble, you did not do for me.' In the little parable of the two sons, Jesus knew well enough that men and women often only get round to doing things at the second attempt; he certainly indicated more than once the danger of words without actions to follow.

He certainly calls us to action, and action for and with our neighbours. The parable of the Good Samaritan was told in illustration of the summary of the law 'Love God and love your neighbour', and his refusal to let the second part be rationalized away. Jesus again pointed his contemporaries to the society in and around them as the place where God called for them to be involved. There can be no escape into loving God apart from our neighbours. The love of our neighbour doesn't exhaust our love of God, but it cannot be divorced from it.

As we have thought, growth in prayer begins with that deeper looking at Jesus and his words which has immediate implications for our behaviour. Jesus is never content with a subjective reaction; he speaks of doing, or external action, of involvement. For most people the main involvement will be through their work. It is important not to overlook this very obvious fact, for so many switch off attention to God when they go to work. In the case of some this is due to the pressure of the indifference to God which they experience amongst those they work with; perhaps embarrassment would be a better word than indifference, and this is often worth probing. For others, the switching off comes through their absorption with work, and their concern to make a success of it. Both groups need to see work as part of the conversation with God, which is indeed a three-sided conversation of God, our neighbours and ourself. This conversation with God, or calling or vocation, has too often been confined within narrow limits, to the priesthood, teaching, medical or social work. It would be a strange and difficult world if God had only intended these kinds of work. We need to see that the three-cornered conversation can involve all kinds of work.

For some the choice of work will be very limited by circumstances of family needs or national economy, of upbringing and abilities. Others will have a wide choice; they need to weigh the claims of others and family and the claims of God, and his possible particular use of them, as they try in prayer to enter into this three-cornered conversation. Yet even those with very limited choice can still get help from making the conversation with God explicit, day by day. Gradually they may come to see some use in the job, or at least in their relationships within it. They have to face their own needs both to work and to earn their families' sustenance. They can gradually discern something of the call of God, maybe to bear that job for a time, and then look for another, or to carry it as their part in sharing the load of the world.

Many of these latter will find a great part of their fulfilment from getting involved in outside voluntary work. Here they can find the support of a more congenial group, who share their concern for the world and for God. At the same time, those who are happily absorbed in their work have their need to look outside; they need to see the wider perspective of God's care for all, and some piece of voluntary work may be their best way of doing this. They will find further help from being involved in a mixed group from very different working backgrounds. Those whose work is very heavily involved with people may have little time, or emotional energy, for further involvement. This is fair enough, but they may be very valuable to voluntary groups with advice and help from time to time. These people will need all the more the general corporate life of the congregation in the church to give them balance and support.

Involvement may come through one of the caring groups; we have many models to follow these days. There are the Fish schemes of neighbourhood service, which originated from a parish group and has spread to wider circles; there are local groups of the national movements such as the Samaritans, Shelter, Age Concern, to name a few. You don't have to look very far to find a group, or on the other hand, advice and literature if you want to start a group yourself.

Involvement in local need will point some to the necessity of political action at either local or national level. This can be a real leading or part of the growth of prayer. Though it is certainly true that political action stirs and uses a good deal of ambition and aggression, we have to face the fact that in all areas of life motives are nearly always mixed. If a society is to live together it must have political action, and in large societies this necessarily takes some party form. We need people in politics and in parties who are aware of the mixture of motives but who have some outside point of reference and association, some transcendent critique. They also need an ability to cope with the mixture, and the disappointment and the failures of life. They need to know something of forgiveness and grace. This is just as true of people involved in any local helping group, or indeed, in any work situation. Personalities and passions can run high; we all need the outside point of reference and critique. We need the outside association; we need, in fact, involvement with our fellow Christians, with Christ and his grace.

We begin to understand why Jesus formed his followers into a group. He chose twelve close followers to be the fathers of the new Israel. He knew how God had worked through Israel to gather men into a family. He had taken hold of Abraham and his family, as they grew up into a closely related nation. Jesus' followers were to be the first instalment of a wider fellowship for all nations. They had some hesitations about this wider task at first, but Paul soon helped the church to get clear that it was for Gentile as well as Jew. He discovered he had to sort out some simple human egoisms and divisions amongst Gentiles in Corinth, and in the letter to them which appears as our I Corinthians he drew that vivid picture for them of our relationship to Christ through the Spirit implying that we are limbs of his body. This is no theoretical picture, we need to see the closeness of our involvement, one with another, in Christ, that we are part of a truly corporate life.

Christians have argued down the centuries whether the corporate life of the church is meant to be visible, or can only be invisible. As in most arguments, there is a truth on both sides. Christ invites us to worship God at his table – 'Do this in remembrance of me' he said. So Christians have found their worship centred in communion; indeed here they have found that their corporate life as the body of Christ is built up as they feed on Christ It doesn't end there, it is to be expressed in all sorts of ways At its simplest it continues in cups of coffee or tea after worship; it may become elaborated to various social functions. There needs to be in between, an opportunity for some groups, informal or more formal, to discuss, to learn, to give some real exchange and support. A Christian congregation or a neighbourhood need to express their responsibility to the world around and afar, both in communicating Christian understanding of God, and also in expressing God's love and care for all men. Part of this task has to be left to individual Christians in their own lives, but there should be some corporate awareness and discussion of these responsibilities.

This may be too much for some to organize in the local neighbourhood or parish, where resources may be limited, so the church is moving towards a greater consciousness of wider areas, in some kind of group or circuit or deanery, in which it should be possible to provide some exchange and discussion. This also enables more corporate involvement in the national life of the church, and should help people to see their involvement in society at large; through the international life of the church we can experience something of it on a world scale. We need to see that these are not just organizations for their own sake, but the means by which Christians can be involved in the world at large. We need to keep ourselves aware, and in this way participating in this involvement, through books and papers.

All this can help to take us out of ourselves. The local group at the church, odd and difficult though it may seem to us, can give us an immediate awareness of the claims and difference of other people, and our need to be shaken out of ourselves. The present moves towards larger local units can shake us out of too cosy a local concern. The claims of the world wide mission of the church can stir us out of our provincialism, as can the challenge of new writing and thinking. These will all help our possibility of being useful to others.

We need to contribute to others, as they do to us. We are stirred to serve others by their immediate needs. In the process we may discover that this is very satisfying to ourselves and become uncomfortably aware of our mixed motives. The others won't want us to stop caring for them. Yet it is true that in our involvement with our neighbours in the church we generally begin by thinking very much 'What do we get out of it?' This is indeed very important to us, but we also need to be thinking what we contribute to the church, and how we share in its love of God and love of neighbour.

We need to think what we contribute to worship. This begins with actual thought and attention in worship. It ought to go further than this, to our thinking and talking with others about our common responsibility as the people of God in a place, and about what we ought to offer together, both on Sundays and weekdays. We should think what particular part we as individuals should take in it. We need to think, also, of how we contribute to the wider life of the church. If there is no group in our congregation, why shouldn't we be the one to start? If there is no outreach from the community, either in evangelism or service, we can make a start, and collect others to share with us.

'I don't want to get too involved' may be the reply at this point, and it may continue 'I have so much to do.' This may, indeed, be true, particularly for a person, as we have thought, with a job in which he or she is heavily involved with people and has long hours, or for someone who is heavily committed in political action. This person needs assuring that that is very much part of their Christian involvement; it may be a very large part. He or she will need support and interest from Christian friends and clergy and sometimes balance and judgment. For some it will be a question of being helped gradually to unwind from too limited an involvement, to bring their timetable under the criticism of the gospel, and to reach out wider. For others still it will be a question of being helped through the fear of involvement, out of themselves, into a real relationship with others. For both these there will be great help in a congregation or in a group. For all there is the need of the getting out of themselves into the perspective of worship, and of regular renewal, for this is all part of the process of growing up and out of ourselves, to God and our neighbour.

15 *Renewing*

We are all conscious today of the need of renewal. Our kind of economy has made it a necessity to replace goods at regular intervals, so much so that people are beginning to question whether it's not the economy that needs renewing. In many ways we are conscious that society needs renewing, and its various institutions. We are aware that the church needs renewing but we can take some comfort from the fact that just as society has had its recovery from a dark age, a renaissance, an enlightenment, an industrial revolution, so the church has had its reformation, and various revivals both before and after that, and these have themselves played a big part in the renewing of society.

These renewals, economic, social and religious, are reflected in the individual. We certainly need to renew our clothes and possessions, but need to use some discrimination in doing this. We need physical renewal in food and sleep, and need discrimination here not least to make sure the renewal is of our whole person, and not just of our emotions, though it is very important that our imagination should be renewed. Yet it is important, too, that there should be real content in the renewal of will and action. We must be renewed in our spiritual energy, in our temper, our ideals and our hopes.

It is just at this point that Christian worship offers to take us out of ourselves, both imaginatively and realistically, to cause us to look through the world around us to the transcendent vision of life with God; but also it calls us to the practical demands of God in Christ, and offers us company and help in doing this. It offers this specifically in the content of a new start for a new week; this is not accidental. Sunday became the day of worship for Christians because it celebrated the resurrection of Christ on the first day of the week, and they found in this the possibility of a new start for a new week.

There is more to it than that. Christian worship is not just stopping to remember God once in a while, or even once a week, not just a matter of stopping to remember God as revealed in Christ, particularly in his resurrection. It is sharing in his resurrection, in communion with him. So, as we have seen, Christian worship has centred in the eucharist, the thankful celebration of Christ's death and resurrection, the grateful participation in communion with him, 'the Lord's service on the Lord's day', as John Wesley put it. It is significant that each great renewal in the church has brought the church back to weekly communion. We live in such a time of renewal today.

In communion we are taken out of ourselves, into the wider action of God in Christ. Though we may rightly choose to fashion and reform the prayers that we make in doing this, we are called to take part in an act of Christ's devising. In it he both renews us with his life, and also enables us to share in his offering of himself to his Father, to share in his worship. It is not surprising, therefore, that Christians try to express the act of communion in worshipful ways, with movement and music, and colour. Particular ways will vary with particular tastes, but the worshipful intent is universal. It is not surprising that Christians, from the beginning, have prefaced the act of communion with readings from the scriptures and preaching, to try to understand more of the mind and intent of Christ. This goes right back to Luke's account of the resurrection, and the appearance of Christ at Emmaus 'where he opened the scriptures' and 'was made known to them in the breaking of bread' (Luke 24.32 and 35). The changing scriptures, week by week, give a new and particular point to the act of communion.

Each must take the point to him or herself. Many faithful Christians miss the renewal of communion because they have not been helped to think through the action and the ways of taking this to themselves through preparation. There are points enough to be learned from Christ's words at the Last Supper (I Cor. 11.23-26; Matt. 26.26-28), and we may usefully pick up, at any rate, three. First there are the words 'This is my body; this is my blood.' Here we have the thought of the real gift of Christ of himself; they can have been barely comprehensible to the disciples at the time. Yet through their experience of the risen Christ, coming and going by his own will, when he was taken from them in visible form and the spirit brought understanding, they could begin to see how he could give himself to them in the way he had promised. So 'they broke bread with gladness'. You can see from Paul's first letter to the Corinthians how realistically he takes the gift of Christ in communion, and how important he thinks it is that we 'discern the Lord's body'. It is a wonder indeed; perhaps the church has been too long arguing over the means of Christ's presence, and not sufficiently appreciated his gift of himself. Thankfulness is the sure way to appreciate this.

Christ gives himself not just for company's sake. He gave himself freely in response to his Father and in answer to the need and the selfishness of men and women. His giving ended in death, in the trustful handing over of life itself. He was clearly pointing forward to this when, on the night before he died, he gave his disciples the bread and the wine, saying they were his body and blood 'for you, and for many, for the remission of sins'. The broken bread prefigured his body to be broken, and the wine his blood to be poured out. He was giving them his life given in sacrifice for them and the world. His resurrection vindicated this, and completed the action. So it was on the first day of the week that Christians celebrated this, sharing in his offering of himself, his dying and rising, for the sake of the world. So they saw communion as a call to renew the basic act of sharing in baptism by repentence and faith; communion calls us afresh to die to selfishness and to rise to share Christ's life of free giving. Repentance and faith, or trustful looking forward, form the response to this sharing in the sacrifice of Christ.

But this is not a private arrangement. Jesus gave his disciples this way of sharing in himself 'for you, and for many', sharing in the new covenant, in his blood. He gives himself, indeed, for the renewal of all people, and indeed all things, to draw them together into a great union and covenant with God. As we share in communion with him we are drawn into communion with others. It is in fact just at this point that the church has often found the challenge of Christ too great. Various disagreements have caused Christians to divide and to break off sharing communion one with another. Christian unity is not an extra, however, but an essential part of communion with Christ. Thus disunity is not just a product of institutions; it stems from a deep tendency in people not to take responsibility for others, so Paul had to teach his Corinthian converts their interdependence in the body of Christ 'We, being many, are one body, for we all partake of the one bread.'

We need to learn this at a deeper level than we realize, not only by a real concern for Christian unity, but by a real change of attitude. We still tend to think and talk of 'my' communion when it is clearly 'our' communion with Christ and with each other. We can help ourselves do this if we see that we must be thinking and praying with other people, we need to give thought to our particular intercessions, as we come to communion. We also need to give thought to the way in which we join in the prayers and the action with others. Quite rightly, much of our thinking about reforming our liturgy is concerned with ways of helping people participate and do things together, not least by singing and by actions. Though these are easy to do with a small, closely knit body, it's all the more important to find ways of sharing together in a larger body, which is open to people coming and going. This is helped by some opportunity to meet, perhaps for refreshment after the communion service; this is really a vital part of the participation in worship. This is not just a chore and a matter of organization; indeed, part of seeing the corporate nature of communion is seeing that it is concerned with chores and organization. It is significant that Jesus gives us himself through food and drink, you might say through the products of man's labour, and through the things of the kitchen too. So sharing with Christ in communion can remind us that Christ shares in the world, and our work and circumstances; our preparation and participation in prayer ought to include some thought and prayer about our work and our circumstances about the world around us.

We can gather up from these three lines suggested by the words of Christ (and there are no doubt many others), three, or rather four points of prayer – thanksgiving, repentance and resolution, and intercession for people and for causes. Before communion on Sunday it is quite simple to gather such thoughts up over the past week. We can see what we have to thank God for, what we need to die to, and what we hope to rise to, and then for whom and what, outside ourselves, we ought to pray – and we can take all these into our communion. The thanksgiving can widen out, as we have seen, from the good things that have happened to us, to take in the good things that we have been able to do and share in. The penitence can go on from the obvious failures to the deeper attitudes and resistances, particularly the fears and hesitations to which we cling. The resolution should not be so much to make a great attempt, often desperate, to do better; rather it should spring from a realization that this is what Christ wants to do in us, and so trust that we can try to do it in communion with him. The intercession can include people and causes with particular needs, but also those pieces of work and difficult circumstances that confront us in daily life.

The centre of this praying is very much the sharing in the dying and rising; our thanksgiving and our intercession revolve around these two. The words of Christ giving us a share in the dying and rising provide us with a constant way of renewal. This sharing renewal can be very obvious over a week when communion can give us a realistic new start for a new week. Such a sharing can also be a help on a week day; it may be a day with some special task. As we think further about relating the days to God using one or more days during the week to lift up the daily round of the working week in communion, there is another obvious point in lifting up a day in celebration of a personal joy, of a birthday or anniversary; this points to the sharing in the church's birthday parties of the saints' days in communion. We need a good deal more of this joy and celebration, in the church and in the world. For a weekday communion the preparation can be simply by a deepening of the evening prayer the night before, in its usual parts, with some particular thought and intention for the following day.

Before a Sunday communion, the longer look over the week will have obvious practical uses. It may be a help to some to make a brief note with a pencil and paper; this can help us to be definite in thinking at the time. It can also clarify prayer during the actual act of communion. It may also give some idea of the movement of our lives over the weeks. God is certainly on the move with us; he calls us to move with him. He asks us to look deeper, but also to reach out further. Christ offers us himself so that we can go forward with him in communion by constant renewal.

16 *Probing*

Constant renewal may seem to some a contradiction in terms; this is an offer which requires some probing. It certainly does, but it is we who require the probing. The need for self-criticism gradually comes home to us as we gather thoughts from meditation on the gospels or elsewhere, particularly through those thoughts which make us explore our attitudes. Further points are brought home to us in looking back over the week in preparation for communion; some of these points are brought home week after week, which begins to make us think that we really ought to do something about them, that we should, in the first place, do some longer term stocktaking and accounting.

We ought to do this accounting on both sides. It is certainly true that the consciousness in our prayer over the weeks shows us there is much to be thankful for, as well as a good deal to be sorry for. There is much to encourage us, and we ought to take this in; it gives us the assurance that God will lead us further, that he can take us on through a deeper probing of ourselves to a truer relationship with him. It is a good plan, therefore, to stop and think and thank from time to time, or, we might say, from term to term; for we all have terms, whether they come from education or business or seasons. We can very usefully gather up thanksgiving for what has happened to us, and what has happened in us over the last few months. It will be more than we think, and it may be well worth while working it out on a piece of paper, just to take in how much there is to be thankful for.

This thanksgiving gives us a very simple means of understanding a little of that basic redemption of the world in Christ we thought of earlier, 'plentiful redemption', as Fr Faber's hymn says. Thanksgiving shows us that God really does do something with us, odd and insignificant mixtures of people though we are. We can therefore trust that God will do more with our mixture, for nothing is too big or too petty for him to sort out; the pettiness, particularly, needs noting. We often make the mistake of thinking that we are really too much in the petty preliminary stage for God to bother. 'When I've sorted things out, I might get going.' We're rather like the Irishman in the old Punch story 'If I were going there, I wouldn't be starting from here.'

But the fact is we do start just here, and so, too, does God. This is what the incarnation means; God works here in human life. He worked in the particular life of Jesus; of Jesus as he met the ordinary mixture of men and women, and met death at their hands. Then the disciples discovered that through his resurrection and the gift of the Spirit he could still be with them in power, to sort men out, to absolve, to forgive, those mixed up men, and to work through them to go out and touch and change, and sort out, men and women of succeeding generations.

This is presented in a nutshell in John's gospel's account of Jesus meeting his disciples on the evening of Easter day. He came to those men shut up behind bars of fear, paralysed by the sense of their own failure. He repeated his greeting of 'Peace'. He showed them his hands and his side, to demonstrate that he really meant all was well, all was forgiven and accepted in his acceptance of suffering in his body. Then he committed to them his Spirit, to take his forgiveness out to men and women. 'Receive the Holy Spirit. Whose sins you forgive they are forgiven them' (John 20.22). This account no doubt comes to us through the musing mind of the author of John's gospel, but all the more it tells us what the first Christians found was true for them from the risen Christ. They found this promise of forgiveness so important, that these words in John's gospel have been used in the ordination of priests from the earliest times to the present.

The church has found this gift of forgiveness almost too good to believe at times, but has learnt to use it by experience. Christians have learnt that God is more forgiving than they had thought, and that men's need of forgiveness was wider than they thought. The church learnt there is more forgiveness than the initial act of baptism; it learnt, too, that we need forgiveness not only for the big acts of murder, adultery and apostasy, but also for everyday acts and attitudes. At the Reformation the reformed churches learnt to make specific confession and absolution an option, rather than a matter of rule. Since then, Anglicans and others have learnt, with all the danger of neglect that this option has given us, to take the offer in a more positive way. Indeed, some of the most interesting thinking about the use of specific absolution has come from Protestant sources, such as the community at Taizé, where Max Thurian has written a valuable little book *Confession and Absolution*, and the English Methodist Neville Ward in his notable book *The Use of Praying*.

The brothers at Taizé say that though they find Christians often have a general sense of God's forgiveness, they do not always think how, or whether, they can get hold of it. They very much need help for this specific act. This is part of our response to the particularity which runs all through the Bible to the particular person of Christ; it meets our need to be helped to start from just where we are, with our individual peculiar mixture. To help us God chooses to use the ministry of particular men, and we are helped to express ourselves in words to another person. Though we may be helped a great deal in the process of coming out of ourselves in a group, we normally find that the deepest level is reached with one other person, in confidence. In using the help of a priest to make a specific confession you might say we combine the pair and the group; for we become very conscious that we are in the presence of God. The part of the priest will be to help us to see what God is saying and doing. Yet the talking and listening do help us to focus our attention. For most of us it is part of this particularity that one particular priest will help us more than others. For most people this will be someone they know, or get to know, well; for others it will be someone from whom they are more detached. The church has always recognized this; the 1662 Prayer Book says 'Come to me, or to some other . . . minister of God's word.'

When we begin to see there is some point in probing deeper for us, we are reminded of Jesus' picture of the Father coming down the road to meet us to help us to come to ourselves – to our senses and to him. This is the point to ask consciously for the help of the Holy Spirit who, as John's gospel puts it. 'Will convict the world of sin, of righteousness and of judgment' (John 16.8). This is one of the places at which to discover that the prayer for the help of the Holy Spirit is not just a formality He can really get us thinking and acting. We need to use our minds to follow his stirring. Sometimes, the awareness comes tumbling out; we need then to sort it out, and see it in order, and to probe further to see what lies behind it. At other times we have a more general idea, and need some help to look at it particularly. There is help ready to hand in the Bible; very obviously there is the list of the Ten Commandments (Ex. 20), or perhaps more to the point, the Sermon on the Mount (Matt. 5,6 and 7), where the commands of the law in their negative form are turned round, and driven home in their positive form. Again there is that very positive list of the fruits of the Spirit, in Galatians 5.22 'Love, joy, peace, long-suffering, kindness, goodness, faithfulness, meekness, temperance'. These give you their help to look at different atitudes and habits of life. It will be well worth looking at these, either after the first stirring or at the start, to start you thinking.

It will certainly help to have a pencil and paper; this helps us not only to gather our thoughts, but to put them in some order, and to begin to see them objectively, in black and white. This will also help us to work out what are the causes when we look at ourselves in this deep way for the first time. We begin to say 'Well, I've always been like that', and remember 'I was like that, so I did that.' It's simpler, therefore, to look at life in stages, maybe childhood, adolescence, adulthood, or the distant past, the recent past, and the immediate period. Some particular acts matter, and need facing, in particular; if we don't face them they tend to fester, and cause remorse. Many acts, of course, don't matter so much in themselves, but in the general attitude and direction they have given to our lives.

We certainly need to look at the things we have failed to do, as well as the things we have done. There is a need to look, too, at fears as well as obvious failures. There is a right and healthy physical fear, there is also anxiety and worry which comes from our deep concern for ourselves.

It should be possible for us to sort things out in this way. For some it will be just a matter of making notes, which we can then express in words; for others it will be a help to think what we mean by writing down what we must say, for in one way or another we need to come to the point and admit where we have failed. In that combination of the pair and the group which we mentioned, in the help of a priest, we can come to the point in the presence of God.

It's a simple matter then to take your paper with you to church, either at a time when confessions are advertised, or at a time specifically arranged. When the priest is ready you kneel beside him at the place indicated; there is generally a card provided to give you a way to introduce your confession. After the priest has given an introductory blessing the card gives an introduction and then you say what you want to from your piece of paper, and anything you wish to add. The card will normally give a conclusion as a simple way of offering this all to God. The priest will then give you counsel, generally now in the form of talking things over; in this feel quite free to ask questions, so that you can see something of what God is working out, and what you can work out. The counsel will end with a penance; that is not a punishment, but a small act of thankfulness to start you on your way. Then the priest gives the absolution, the particular absolution in the second person singular; the Anglican form is found in the service for the visitation of the sick 'Our Lord Jesus Christ, who left power to his church to absolve all sinners who repent, of his great mercy forgive thee thine offences, and by his authority committed unto me I absolve thee from all thy sins. In the name of the Father, and the Son, and the Holy Spirit.'

It's common sense to stay a little time in church to thank God, and to gather up in your mind, and perhaps on paper something of the advice and what you see to work out. You may well go on to work out a little plan for the future, to offer at your next communion. Destroy the self-examination paper – all that can be left with God; he does accept us.

There is an obvious help and fittingness in making a specific confession and receiving absolution in church, but confessions can and do come out in the course of conversation with a priest, it may be in an armchair, it may be on a walk; then counsel and absolution can come out of that conversation on the spot too. God is not confined in his actions: he moves with sovereign freedom but he certainly wants to meet us at the deepest level and knows we need all sorts of help. He will meet us wherever we are.

Part of the power of forgiveness is to make us see deeper. We need to use this power to grow further, through further penitence and forgiveness; sometimes people miss it through shortsightedness. They think, rather over simply, that all should be a steady progress, and are disappointed by their awareness of failure. Their friends are certainly not disappointed; they see real progress in the increased awareness, and we need to see this too. Thanksgiving will save us from being dismal about it, and it will certainly be wise to follow that plan of doing some deeper specific examination and confession something like from term to term.

We often only learn this by default; we may be woken up at some stage, and then, perhaps a year later, realize that nothing much has happened since the first few months. The stirring may have come in Lent, and Christmas is round again before we wake up. Or it may be we were stirred in the autumn, and it's only when the summer holiday approaches that we realize that nothing much has been happening since the spring. The round of the church's year with its reminders of the events of Christ's life offers us various opportunities; Christmas calls us to share in the new life, Easter calls us to a deep dying and rising with Christ. Perhaps it is a compliment to us that God leaves us to find a point in the other two thirds of the year; for many this will be before or after the summer holiday, the end of the summer term, or the beginning of the autumn one. Michaelmas may be a stirring reminder to some to deeper thinking before the season goes further. But one way and another most of us need two or three times in the year to stop, and look deeper, to come to ourselves, and to admit our failings and take hold of God's forgiveness just where we are, and to go on to a new stage with him.

17 *Dying*

'It's all very well, but there's a catch in it somewhere.' So adults echo children; all through life we hear people saying this, some more than others, and catch ourselves saying it too. It is not surprising that some religions have interpreted life in a dualistic way, maintaining an ultimate struggle of powers of good and evil. Christianity has maintained that the snag lies in human responsibility in the use we made of our freedom. This is the meaning of the concept of original sin which runs through the Bible. It is certainly a struggle to deal with it, and it is often more than we can cope with. But this is the struggle which Jesus took on, sharing our life, and took to the cross, in trust, and was raised to share his life and his power with us. So we are called to share the struggle, and the cross, in our lives, and one of the simplest understandings of the cross is to see it is just an 'I' crossed out.

Living with Christ is a process then of dying to self to share life with him. 'There, I told you there was a snag!' Christianity is always talking about death, and writes little crosses over everything. These crosses, however, are not arbitrary; Jesus didn't make his own, he was brought to his death by a combination of human forces. So our little deaths come to us from the combination of human circumstances, as we have thought already, not least as we grow in conversation with God in prayer.

Every act of human attention is an act of self-denial; so the small child has to learn to cut out some sights and sounds and other sense impressions in order to concentrate on the significant ones from the moment he, or she, learns to concentrate on mother. So if we are to grow in relationship with our Father we have to shut out some sense impressions, so that many find it a help to close eyes to sights and ears to sounds in order to pray. However, prayer, like life, soon asks a much wider attention than this; in fact prayer reinforces the demands of life which the other people around us make on our sense of responsibility. We have to learn to say 'no' to ourselves, in order to say 'yes' to other people.

The challenges of self to meet the needs of others, widens out to meet the needs of life; there is a whole fabric of life to be sustained, if we are simply to express ourselves and be there to meet others. These run from getting up in the morning through the chores of home, to the routine of work. It's easy to decry society, institutions, establishments, and to extol the simple life of the spirit. But this is not necessarily the way of the Spirit of God, who made a highly complex world, and gave us power and responsibility to share in its running. It is not necessarily the Spirit of Jesus, who worked for many years in hidden Nazareth; and when he moved out on his mission was prepared to use and to speak about the daily round of life of other people. We all have to submit to the demands of the round of life which both put limits on our freedom and show us the limits of our own abilities.

The most obvious limitation for many of us is time. Though it is true that we all have the same amount of it, for most of us it seems too little. So we are always having to make choices as to how we use that time, what we have time to do and what we have not. It is worth realizing that this is a basic and important part of our human choice. We can either deceive ourselves in rationalization or see what is worth doing and doing it. We must also realize that we have to give up doing some things, good and right in themselves but more than we can do at this particular moment. We all know that in practice we all make time for really important things. On this basis, it ought to be possible for us to make time to pray and to worship: in fact it will be a simple way of showing we think God important. In fact it is a very real way of finding God and finding who he really is.

This choice of time of course involves saying 'no' to other things. It is obvious that saying 'no' to self is a very pointed act of saying 'yes' to others and to God. It can help us face the rightful demands that others make on us for our attention. We have to choose to which demand we respond. We shall know that some are very rightful and we may suspect that God is very interested in our response. Some of these demands will be repeated to us again and again, and we shall want to act on them. We may find it a help to offer to Christ some particular acts as a steady minimum; perhaps something we do each week in the way of service to others or to him, or our simple self denial to enable these things. The Christian tradition of some form of self denial on Fridays has an obvious point in linking this with the agony of Christ. It also has a very simple practical advantage in enabling us to do something before the week has ended. This may point us back to make sure that we really meet our obligations and chores in life before we go on to other things. However small these token acts may be, they are not negligible or negative; they can be the material on which we fashion a new attitude, to be able to offer ourselves to life in a freer and less detached way.

As we have thought already, this saying 'no' to ourselves is no arbitrary or artificial attitude; we are challenged to it by the demands of life, as Jesus was challenged to the cross. It is put to us by every simple argument or disagreement, in the family or amongst friends. Are we simply going to hold on to our own position, and make sure we get our way, or have we got sufficient awareness and practice of saying 'no' to ourselves to let something pass, and to think of the other's interest before our own? These are not small matters; they may be the making or breaking of a marriage. They are questions which come up in the family life, or in the family life of the church. The questions are becoming increasingly complicated with size, in work and politics, where they need all the more men and women to grow up and out of themselves. Certainly in these large and more complicated fields there is great need for us to discuss and have the support of some outside group. This is the support that Christians ought to be able to give and to receive, built on humble honesty in which we can see our own weakness and failure, and yet know that the way ahead is not by self justification but by trust in God's justification, which is ready to go out of self, to serve others.

This attitude is often most tested over questions of handing over jobs and status. Even when we hand over a piece of work in order to take up a more exciting one we part with part of ourselves. So, too, when we have to delegate some part of our work because we have other things to do, we naturally find a difficulty in parting with something we have built up. It is easy to see the need for this in the case of other people, but we find it difficult for ourselves. The company of Christ should certainly help us directly here, to see that these little deaths can be ways of living more fully, for him and for others. We ought to be able to find this help even when the handing over is not of our choosing, and means an obvious loss of place or payment. Though immediately this seems to render us less useful, we need to trust God to use this way of denial, as Christ trusted his own immobilization on the cross, after his busy ministry. We may get no further than seeing that other people respect and appreciate the way we stepped down, but we can trust God that it will bear long term fruit.

The fact we know now, that Jesus did his greatest work in the painful restriction upon the cross can, of course, be the greatest help to those who are literally laid aside by injury or illness. It may be a help for them to pray quite literally to share Christ's yearning on the cross. They can discover that when pain makes thinking almost impossible they can simply offer the pain; this can be a very real way of sharing both his pain and the pain of the world.

For some, retirement may be a very welcome relief, but for others it may indeed be worse than sickness. At its simplest, it can be a time to accept that we are not indispensable; this is true not only negatively, but also positively, meaning that we are at God's disposal. We can then offer ourselves to him to be used in whatever ways are presented to us. This will certainly include looking out for ways to be used, but not forcing ourselves on people, or trying to make ourselves indispensable again. Retirement can be a time to grow further in being less possessive about life. Of course there are temptations for people at this time to become more anxious about their human needs. Our training of prayer in trust and letting go ought to be used here, even to the extent of not being anxious about doing all the things we want to in prayer, facing our limitations of concentration, and being prepared to trust ourselves simply into his hands.

The great handing over, of course, is death. Though it presents the demands of life in an ultimate way, it also can call out the most direct attention to God. As Dr Johnson is said to have put it, to know he has only a few hours to live 'wonderfully clears a man's mind'. Of course this depends on people knowing something of the likelihood of death while they are still conscious; psychiatrists are helping doctors today to see through the conspiracy of silence. Though some patients apparently do not forsee their deaths, many more do, though they may not talk about it. There is a great need to be able to help people share the prospect of death in a positive way. Christians ought to be able to help people, and themselves, with this, if they have been learning something in prayer of the way God helps us to grow up and out of ourselves, to others and to himself.

The last stages of a life can be made very positive by gathering up the growth that has gone before; this will often be in a simple way of meeting friends and relations, recalling past happiness, handing over fears and failures for God's forgiveness. Dr Cicely Saunders has made notable studies of this gathering up of life in her work with terminal patients at St Christopher's Hospice in South London. Of course, sudden death, on the roads for instance, will prevent all this. This can only remind us of the prior need to understand the positive line of handing ourselves to God and dying to self, which runs all through life. This is no arbitrary line, but one demanded by life; it is often implicit before it is made explicit in a person's life. It may, in fact, be in a time of sudden death that those left can be helped to see that this handing over was going on in the life that was cut off, and has begun for them, and can go on further.

The gate of death certainly brings us to the gate of faith, which we have looked at earlier. Again we ask 'But is there really anything the other side?' Again the reply is to discover that faith doesn't lie so much in an intellectual projection into the future, but in coming to terms with life and God in the present. The Christian hope of life beyond death is certainly based on the conviction that Jesus Christ was raised from the dead. It is based on more than this, however, it is based on the possibility of being able to share that risen life with Christ here and now, through the operation of the Holy Spirit. It is interesting to see how Paul's thinking about the future life of Christians fills out, as his life goes on. In I Corinthians 15 he can put courage into Christians who have lost their friends with the picture of the seed growing into corn. He still thinks he will be alive at the end of the world, though he realizes that those alive must then be changed. Between writing this and our II Corinthians we gather Paul had nearly died himself (II Cor. 1.8), and so in II Corinthians 5 he has to approach the question of death in a much more existential way. However, he can trust God, even with his own death; he knows God has already given him what he calls the 'first instalment or pledge of the Spirit'.

Paul was well aware that his human body was only flesh; he didn't think that he had an immortal spark in himself, because he knew that response to God and self-concern were still mixed up in himself. Yet he believed that God could cope with human failure and death, as he had shown in the resurrection of Jesus; he trusted God would raise him to new life. Furthermore, he was very clear as a Jew that this must be whole human life, expressed as an embodied person; he didn't mean the restoration of the physical body, but the raising to be an embodied spirit, or a spiritual body. This is what he had meant in I Corinthians 15.52, in that triumphant conclusion used so effectively in

Handel's Messiah: 'The trumpet shall sound, and the dead shall be raised incorruptible, and we shall be changed.'

The New Testament at one place indicates that it can't say more about this future life, except that we can begin to understand it from our present relationship to Christ, and the life in the Spirit. We may perhaps have a simple understanding of this if we stop for a moment to realize how our relationship with God affects our behaviour at present. It stirs our stumps, it makes us lend a hand, and at times opens, and at others, shuts our mouths. In fact it produces a kind of spiritual nervous and muscular system. Furthermore, we are rightly dubious about a person's relationship with God unless it shows itself in these physical ways. Don't we begin to see something here of the spiritual body? Of course we are very aware that it's very incomplete at present, and needs some radical change and completion. Yet our experience here encourages us to think that in spite of our partial response God has been making the going, and we can hope that he will complete it after death.

The Bible encourages us to think that God does things thoroughly, as it were from the bottom upwards, so it looks to us more likely that this completion after death will be in some sense a process, and not instantaneous. There is a good deal in the Bible about purification, purging, and this had led the main Christian tradition to think that for most of us there is a process of purification or purgation after death. It's unfortunate that pessimistic ideas have often been foremost, and led to lurid pictures of purgation; it's not surprising that men reacted from these at the Reformation. Unfortunately, they reacted in the way of posing instantaneous perfection for the elect, and damnation for the rest. We can see that both those are wrong; though present ideas of time must end with death, much in the New Testament points to a process after death, and it certainly encourages us to see that God's judgment is much more generous than ours. It's interesting that the parable which carries the highest degree of colouring about judgment, quite likely added in the later telling of it, the Sheep and the Goats (Matt. 25.31-

46), is about this reversal of ideas about judgment. Heaven is not for those who thought they made all the right answers, but do not open their hearts to others, but the generosity of God is there for those who didn't think they had done anything for God, but have opened their hearts to others.

In this and other remarks of Jesus it looks as though this opening yourself to others and thereby really to him, is basic. This is what opens us to relationship with him in the Spirit, and it is through this that God will call us into new life with Jesus, and eventually to perfection. Once again it seems likely that God respects absolutely the freedom he has given us to choose to use relationship with him. If we really want to shut ourselves up in ourselves, and not come out to others we can, but if we do so what will we really have when the body perishes? Probably nothing, and the New Testament colouring of fire and destruction is a picture of this nothingness.

The element of dying that runs through life certainly poses an ultimate question to us. It is the question of whether we live to ourselves, or reach out of ourselves to others and to God. If we see every demand on us from the circumstances of life and other people, from the stages of development, in negative terms, as a threat to our self possession, we shall in the end be left with nothing. On the other hand, we can face each of these demands, and in spite of our hesitations find them to be stages of growing up out of ourselves. If we are wise we shall take note of this and get into a certain amount of practice about it, so that we can face the little and the big losses in life, and the final loss of life and all time; and to find a way of growing up and out of ourselves in relationship to others and to him.

18 *Living*

Is life ultimately a tragedy? Do death and self denial have the last word? These are recurring questions, but to confine one's attention to them is profoundly to misunderstand Christian faith; for what makes faith specifically Christian is Christ and his resurrection. Though Jesus faces us with the cross and the need for self surrender, even of life itself, he also presents us with God's affirmation of his power to raise and restore life. So the heart of relationship with God, the heart of prayer, is always to say 'yes' to God, and as we have thought, yes to our neighbour, and yes to his creation. If we reach out to God with Jesus Christ we know we reach out to the Father, who not only makes and sustains life, but also redeems its failures, and goes on renewing and inspiring it.

Certainly, this has not seemed very obvious at many times in the church's history. It was not surprising that Christianity appealed to men and women by its other-worldliness. You can see the strength of this appeal in the persecutions, both of the early centuries and later. It was there in the rise, and the repeated return of monasticism, and since the Reformation it has been present in individual piety, Protestant, Catholic, Orthodox. Yet the world has discovered also that Christian other-worldliness has always had a very worldly concern with it, for the church which weathered the persecutions took over the administration of the Roman empire, the monks became the great agents of social care, the evangelicals the pioneers of slavery and factory reforms. Though by fits and starts, Christianity has shown itself to be concerned with both love of God and love of neighbour.

Nowadays, the commonest reaction is to a this-worldly religion, with a laudable concern to care for the neighbour, for justice, carried to an extreme, so that some maintain that love of God can only be pursued through the love of neighbour, and that worship is only a means to this end. Though this appears to be a very affirmative way, emphasizing the joy of life and society, it is likely to be in the end a negative way. It has to deny and shut its eye to all sorts of things, not only to much human experience of God in worship and mysticism, but also to much of the difficulty of life, to the rejection of love and care, even by those at the receiving end, to the waste and failure of good effort. The proponent of this-worldly religion has to shut his eyes to much hardship and suffering, and of course to death itself. We need a religion which can put together death and life, this-worldliness and other worldliness, and to rediscover the paradox of Jesus which has kept the church alive.

It is clear that the religion which is built on the belief that God has shown himself in a human life is bound to be concerned with life. Relationship with God in Christ in prayer does not mean a separate life, though some have made it appear very like this. It has to cope with the whole of life, not just the great moments, but also the petty and frustrating ones, the disappointments and the failures. This means the prayer of renewal and redemption will be particularly important, to remind us of Christ's power to raise and restore. Some of the simple practices of prayer are particularly significant here, as they relate us with Christ, and his claim to cope with the whole of life and death. The simple practice of praying in the morning as well as the evening can give us a reminder of the raising to new life. Our view of life looks better and clearer in the light of morning. We can thank God for this and make use of it; we can look further in hope, reminded that God raises us not only from sleep but from failures and fear, and can raise other people, and his world too. We have already thought how communion can give reinforcement and substance to the beginning of the week on Sunday morning. It can give us a new start to the week in the assurance that we have renewed and strengthened our relationship with Christ in his dying and rising, and redeeming of life. So we can pray and care with renewed conviction for his continuing work for redemption in the world. We know it does not end there; we go out from communion in continual relationship with him and to find him at work in his world.

We need to be looking for this. It is all too easy to confine God to his church, his sacraments, to prayer; it is also a danger to confine him to the crises of life, to sickness, death and failure. But God is not to be so confined; he is the Lord and sustainer and redeemer of it all, all the time. Furthermore, it is in the day to day and moment by moment living of life that our life is being continually made and remade, and the lives of those around us, so the relationship with God is to be worked out moment by moment. This thought has led various men and women of prayer to find a particularly vivid reminder in that text from St Paul 'Pray without ceasing'. It was the starting point of the classic of the nineteenth-century Russian spirituality *The Way of a Pilgrim* translated into English by R. M. French which is one of the most readable accounts of the Jesus prayer. This is the kind of phrase that can come easily to the mind and can be repeated silently in time with breathing to help us to find a relationship with God, not only in the crises but also in the moment to moment moves of life. Another classic treatment of this point is of course, that of Brother Lawrence, in *The Practice of the Presence of God* telling how he found prayer in his work in the kitchen, albeit in a monastery; the relationship of prayer is not to be confined to a few moments of life, nor to a favoured few, but is for all moments, for all people. It is not very difficult to translate Brother Lawrence from the kitchen to the factory.

Trying to relate life moment to moment to God sounds splendid, but of course raises all the big questions continuously. Is there any real significance in many of the moments which we can relate to God or call good? The best treatment for this is to be found in the unlikely form of the eighteenth-century Jesuit J. P.

de Caussade's letters to nuns. He taught them that fulfilment was not to be found through an anxious striving after complicated practice, but by the 'sacrament of the present moment' and by responding with what he called 'abandonment to divine providence'. These two great phrases are worth studying. All our thinking about relationships and prayer should encourage us to look for God's presence at the present moment. It may be in the form of an opportunity which is not obvious at first; it may be some revelation of the good in someone else. If we look harder we shall often find God's personal concern within each moment; we can catch glimpses of Jesus, and indeed find within it the gift of himself, his sacraments. At the same time we learn by experience that our response to God is not only in greater attention to him but in greater sensitivity. This asks of us a mixture of activity which often baffles us. We seem to be asked to be more thoughtful and at the same time to become more and more pragmatic. We are asked to receive, to grasp 'the sacrament of the present moment' and to move from moment to moment, to look for nothing less than 'abandonment to divine providence'.

These two little phrases serve as a very good signpost on the way. We cannot ask for many signposts beyond this, but we know that they are not the end of the road, but very much signs on the continuing way. That way continues in company of God, ever present and personal, given to us in Jesus, through his Spirit. Those two signposts may indicate some fundamental directions or attitudes that help us to go forward trustfully with him.

Those two phrases might be further expanded with Paul's three words: faith, hope and love. We have seen all along how the quest to find prayer is the quest to find God, and raises the questions of faith. Yet we have seen that even to investigate the intellectual question of faith we have to be prepared to try it and see; the 'it' turns out to be a two-way relationship with God, which means coming to terms with ourselves, our limitations and our needs. This is very much the faith of the moment by moment business of living. If you ask about the faith by which people live, they often begin by saying they lack faith in themselves, but this easily leads, of course, to attempts to bolster the self. As we thought before, it is justification by faith we need to rescue us from the ceaseless round of justifying ourselves. Here again we are reminded of the importance of grasping the significance of the death and resurrection of Jesus, of his coping with life and coping with death. We need to grasp it for ourselves, his forgiveness and justification. We need to be able to walk in faith not in euphoric disregard of our limitations, but in a humble acceptance, both of them and God's justification and use of us. We shall not require life to be guaranteed, protected, or ourselves constantly reassured. If we can learn something of this faith, if we can see how he accepts us, we can accept it all.

We shall need to be able to accept life moment by moment, year by year, and in all that unlimited future that stretches there before us. Some people hesitate to meet this and react by shutting their eyes. We need to open our eyes to it, and to that often forgotten fruit of the Spirit that Paul describes as hope. One thing relationship with the risen Christ should certainly do for us is to enable us to see how God can restore and renew, and open new worlds ahead. We know that he can help us to look through our own deaths, and the deaths of our friends and relations; he can help us with the New Testament, to see that he can renew creation; this should give us a deep assurance and hope, to look forward into the infinite future. At the same time we have already thought how hope of life beyond death is based on life with the risen Christ now, so the relationship with Christ in prayer should give us new hope now. The act of intercession for others is an act of hope for them. Every act of prayer for ourselves is an act of hope for ourselves. It is worth recognizing and remembering this, to give us a positive and constructive outlook both in our dealings with other people and with ourselves. It is particularly worth remembering that the Holy Spirit, through whom we pray, gives us this hope in our prayers. So in these moments when all seems dark and we seem to be stuck, we can look forward to God. Though life, work, and circumstances around us may seem to confine us to the old round, God does not leave us to it, he takes us out to new ground in old circumstances.

All the time we can be sure that God is drawing us out towards himself and other people, for he is the God of love. He gives us himself, he gives us his love. It is all too easy to say the word and miss the meaning. This is part of the experience of love, that it goes beyond, and is more generous; we begin to learn it, and as we recognize something of it we respond to God in gratitude. We know we must respond in generosity to others, and find that we go from care to prayer and back again. We find ourselves drawn out to go to God more fully. We know we cannot do this honestly without responding to others more fully, and that means being ready to deny ourselves; and yet to know that this is not negative, but calls us to affirm God more and more.

Still, we know his love is beyond all our affirmation, so we keep on the move, out to God and out to others, to concern, to action, to prayer. Yet God is endless love himself, and calls us, and helps us to respond more and more. Our search is not in vain; as we have thought our search to find God is more of a gradual waking up to the fact he finds us, and then to the fact he holds on to us, distant though he may seem at times. We can know that we are called to respond more and more, not anxiously, but joyfully, delightfully. Joy and delight are two fair expressions of this attitude of love. There must be joy and delight in all God's children, and all God's creations, not overlooking the imperfections and failures, but knowing they are justified in faith and have hope of ultimate redemption. In the meantime it is vital that we should get on with loving them, and we can because he loves us and them. By loving him we shall find out more and more about this and we must yearn to find the way to love him more.

19 *Yearning*

Growth is a process of ups and downs for adults as for adolescents. For adolescents emotions are stirred up into waves and plunged into equally deep troughs, both by the first stirrings of love and by the turmoils of examinations. So too for adults the stages of life bring successive waves, in promotion and success in work, through marriage and child birth and the stages of family growth. These stages also bring the troughs both at work and at home. It is not surprising therefore that we experience the same ups and downs in our relationships with God in prayer, for if this is to grow it must be both integrating and interpreting life both at work and at home. Our prayer is the great work of our life, to make a whole of it, but in a deeper sense it is the great love of life.

We might prefer to say that it should be the great love of life. At times we are carried high on waves of prayer and see the heights of love we want to reach and yearn to be carried there. This is no bad picture; it contains the truth that we are helped to love God by his own ongoing and outgoing love and that we are supported and carried along by him. So our yearning can be hopeful and happy. To be so it will need a strong basic element of trust and also one of humility to realize that we must simply ask God to help us to love him, to serve him adequately, to give ourselves to him, yes, even to trust him more. We can but yearn. It is worth noting that in one of the greatest medieval books on the spiritual life, Jan van Ruysbroek's *The Spiritual Espousals*, the longest of the three sections into which in traditional form he divides his treatment of the spiritual life, is that entitled 'The Life of Yearning for God'. Yearning is certainly a major part of the way in finding prayer and finding God.

We find our way into yearning from various directions. One of the best trodden ways is through the prayer of thinking. We find ourselves returning again and again to thoughts about our response to God. We know this really asks for more love and better temper and trust, and all these seem beyond us; we yearn to be changed and respond in love more fully. All this passes through the mind quite quickly in our prayer, and quite rightly so. There is no need to spend a long time puzzling over resolutions, if we simply realize our need and ask for help, not plaintively but trustfully, lovingly and longingly. We can do this yearning in a simple phrase or two, expressing our need and our longing and our love. We will soon realize that in intimacy few words suffice. It may take us time to find the simple words; we may move from one phrase to another, but using them simply and lovingly and repeatedly may be a very real way of offering our attention and love.

We may come to this yearning kind of praying from a slightly different direction. Our understanding of loving God comes to us very largely through the life and work of Jesus. Looking at the life of Jesus, taking in what he said and did, is a major way to grow in an understanding prayer. We come to find the understanding quicker; in one direction it may lead us on as we thought to thinking about our own needs; in another direction it leads us to admire and love. Before the end this will be beyond our powers; we shall long to love him more and better. We will find again the simple phrases of human love will help us as well as anything; so can the familiar refrains of hymns and poems which have tried to express this love. The old refrain, 'Jesus my Lord I thee adore, O make me love thee more and more', is one such. The section of the Golden Sequence translated as 'Jesus the very thought of thee', is another and there are many more. Writers have not been slow to press into service phrases of the Song of Songs, such as 'he is altogether lovely', and also of the Psalms. The simple repetition of the name 'Jesus' is enough.

The Psalms remind us of another direction leading to the prayer of yearning. For some people, yearning will be for the wider vision of God; they are very conscious of the need to put aside all lesser thoughts, and to give real attention to the one ineffable God. Yet inexpressible as the love of God may be ultimately, they too will find the way to it helped by some directive phrases, both to assist the basic attention and to draw out the love. We hear such yearning in the Psalms themselves, such as 'like as the hart desires the water-brooks', 'Thou art my God, and I will praise thee'. It is not difficult to make a little collection of these phrases. It is useful to have two or three phrases and move from one to another, to offer our attention and love to God.

The techniques of Eastern prayer serve this same purpose of attention. Bodily concentration and relaxation can be a real help to some, especially the restless and the unrelaxed. The repetition of mantras may help to concentrate the mind, as the repetition of Christian phrases, but the words of Christian love are never the murmurings of sweet nothings. What men and women saw of God's love in Christ has given real personal content to the relationship, so we must talk responsibly in personal love to him. Eastern techniques may help some to come to a threshold of awareness, but to stop there may be to stop short of responsibility. This may be an unconscious recognition of the infinite demands of love. The way through lies in the humble trust of yearning.

The prayer of yearning is not to be by-passed with transcendental techniques. In it we work through the layers of self to the deep loving of God. We need the help of simple repeated affective prayer to do this. These short bursts will also be the way to work through the troughs of life, and to discover that they are the further ways of love.

It is not surprising that we also meet troughs of frustration in prayer. The frustration may be the eternal one of lack of time and quiet and privacy; it may also be internal. Though prayer at first seems to become clearer, it often later becomes harder; concentration and the sense of relationship become more difficult. All sorts of questions come crowding in – Is God there? Does prayer work? Why should the world be so full of suffering? All these are questions we thought we had faced and answered before, but now they come back more insistently, and make themselves felt, as it were under the skin.

The truth seems to be that these questions have really to be felt if we are to help ourselves, let alone help others. We can see this truth in the case of other people; we realize that the experience of difficulty and frustration and doubt is an important part of their growing up and maturing. We should not expect to be exempted ourselves. The experience of frustration in prayer can be part of the process of growing deeper into it. We may look back and see how we grew into prayer by breaking through some of the ordinary conditions of life, to find space and time and concentration, and the will to pray. So to grow further in prayer means breaking through the stage of wanting satisfaction, comfort, answers. As has often been said, we have to learn to grow up from praying for our own sakes to praying for God's sake. It shouldn't surprise us that this process goes in fits and starts, so that we pass through periods of waiting when we complain that nothing is happening. We still find this difficult to accept for ourselves, and we react by feeling that we are hard done by. But looking again at other people and their frustrations may convince us that we are not alone. We are certainly not the first Christians to feel this. Writers on prayer down the ages have given vivid descriptions of the frustrating stretches of finding prayer. You can see pictures of this in Jesus in Gethsemane, or Paul in the epistle to the Romans. You will find it in the solitaries in the desert, in the medieval monks and many since. Centuries of Christian prayer return the same answer; we have to grow from praying for our own satisfaction to praying for the whole of God.

One of the most detailed chartings of the way into prayer is given by a sixteenth-century Spanish mystic, John of the Cross. He pictures the difficulty of the way in the imagery of the mountain climb, the Ascent of Mount Carmel. He charts two particular stages of difficulty under the names of the Dark Night of the Senses and the Dark Night of the Soul. We can see these two nights as descriptions of the two stages we have looked at. The first stage is the facing of the difficulty of attention to God in time and place and moral demand; the second comes when the very attention to God seems desperate either to hold or to justify.

John of the Cross gives the further picture of a soul waiting in the frustration of imprisonment. This picture comes straight out of his own experience of being imprisoned by his difficult fellow monks who resented his reforming zeal in a time of laxity and corruption. It is well to realize that the classical writers on prayer wrote out of their own experience of the problems of their day; it may help us to look more closely at the causes of our own frustration. The common ingredient is the opposition to God in the world, which takes different forms in different times and places. In some parts of the world again, as in the early church, it is open persecution. In this country it is much more the dulling effect of indifference, which makes very fair material for frustration. But like John of the Cross too we may share difficulties with colleagues at work, those at home or in the church. In ourselves we face the frustrations of physical exhaustion, maybe ill health. We cannot expect our prayer to be unaffected by these things; indeed if we have found our way any distance into prayer, we shall find that it makes us more sensitive and opens up life so that we feel the effects in one sense all the more. Along this same line we may begin to see that the feeling of frustration is all part of our sharing Christ's caring for the world.

If this is true then, we shall need to look round to see what we can do with the frustration, to look at those relationships at work at home and in the church. Other people certainly make difficulties; we have to see what we can do from our side to sort them out. It may be simply accepting that other people have their problems, but it may also require us to take more positive attitudes and steps ourselves. In the common frustration arising from exhaustion, we need to learn to distinguish the situation, where we must simply accept the load for the sake of others, from other situations where we must learn to resist the temptation to do things for our own personal satisfaction. We have to learn to trust other people and God.

The way through this frustration will involve some awareness of our tendency to be sorry for ourselves. This awareness may come to us apparently rudely from a comment by another person, but we shall find that we need to take it in. Looking at this another way, we see that we have much more than we think for which to be thankful. Another look at thanksgiving may well help us to see some chinks of light through the darkness. It sets us looking in the right direction away from ourselves, towards God, and helps us to turn from being sorry for ourselves, back to being in love with God.

When we turn in this direction, and begin to realize that prayer is for God's sake, and not just for our own, we may very well feel a very long way off from him. It may seem to us that our love for him has to reach to a great distance, and we can barely summon any strength for it. So our prayer must be a prayer of yearning, and a yearning that starts very much from the beginning. It may simply be a prayer to want to pray, and this is fair enough; it may seem almost silly, in actual fact it is humbling. It can certainly begin to open up the situation, and more possibilities for prayer will appear than we thought. As we yearn further, we shall want our prayer to be more realistic, and accompanied by a fuller response in our behaviour and relationships. Though we may feel this is beyond us, so we yearn about these two.

It should not surprise us that the way on through difficulties is both the way of loving, and also the way of application. Sometimes it is a matter of praying to want to pray. This may be a very simple act, but it will need some application. It is a temptation to complain, but if we are really in love with God we shouldn't need application, because love always needs expressing. So we need the acts of prayer, the acts even to want to pray. Classical writers have called these 'forced acts'. The name is unfortunate, but it may remind us of the need at this point; it may also remind us that we can borrow acts from various writers. Classical collections like those in Fr Augustine Baker's eighteenth-century work *Holy Wisdom*, may prove too much for us. However many of the vernacular conversational prayers of recent times have been of this yearning kind. Michel Quoist's *Prayers of Life* have much of this yearning material, as does Rex Chapman's *A Kind of Praying*.

These modern collections remind us forcibly that the process of working through frustration and difficulty is part of our prayer and care for other people; the very feeling of the frustration, and the turning away from self towards God, may be used to help to turn the world away from self-concern and strife towards God. This has often been the experience of people in great physical pain; those in hospital for instance can use their pain simply as prayer for other people in the ward, or for other people across the world. Others too in mental distress or spiritual anguish can be helped to turn outwards to other people in their prayer and care and thought. It can be a great help to have a simple but not overloaded plan of intercession to give us a way of turning away from ourselves day by day. This in turn will help to give us more love and care for God and our neighbour.

There is a clear similarity and continuity between the forced acts and affective prayer; they are both part of this process of growing in prayer, turning out from self towards God and to others; a growing in love and application and attention. This is a middle reach of prayer for most people. In good times it is worth looking for a simple way of yearning with short repeated acts where we dwell for a few minutes on one and then pass to another, and our attention, longing and loving grow. It is a help to have some acts to hand either in mind or on paper or in a book, so that in hard times with such help we can find ourselves carried along on a wave of yearning. As we look for a way through the trough of frustration we find in fact that waves and troughs can be carried by yearning on a strong tide towards God.

20 *Loving*

The deepest things in life are often the most simple. Many of the experiences of finding depth and truth take the form of saying 'of course, I see now, that explains it; I realize I've been dimly aware of it all along'. It all seems so simple, and this is no deception, but the clarity of understanding does take some achievement. It may be thought of as a process of sorting out, of untangling or distilling. The substance has been there all the time, but hidden and ill-defined; we only come to see the wonderful simplicity at the end of a process, often after long effort.

Certainly this is so with prayer; we may see quite early and easily that the heart of it is in loving God. There is much to be done to put that into practice, and many questions to be asked. Does in fact God answer prayer? Why does he allow suffering? Can we help others by our prayers? What about our failures? Each question brings us back to the issue of loving God, but we have to work through to it, and so let our prayer work through to a simpler loving of God. We have known of it in moments before, but as time goes on it becomes more and more the dominant part of prayer, taking other parts in its stride in an obvious way. This may not seem at all obvious to us at a time when life is blank or frustrating in those dark nights. It may be very difficult to believe this love in moments of despair which may come literally in the middle of the night. But as the psalmist puts it – 'Heaviness may endure for a night, but joy cometh in the morning.' As we know from experience that daybreak comes again, we can discover that prayer returns and finds new point and joy in loving God.

This does not necessarily come easily, but there is always some way of working through to a further stage of purification and maturity, a sorting out of our motives, of our concerns, the discarding of a good deal of concern for ourselves and the growth in a simpler concern for God. It requires the effort of concentration; we have looked at one way to this by the use of simple acts of yearning or affection. These phrases serve a double purpose. They help us to reach a greater realism, to yearn about things that matter in our response to God, and they also give us a simple way of concentration. The effort of concentration is a recurrent point in prayer. We tend to dismiss it as just a chore, a burden of our human condition, or a measure of our own disordered lives. It is all these but much more; it is the recurrent call to attend to God, to be devoted, to love him. Turning our attention back again and again to God to a simple text or a repeated phrase or a bare thought and affection, is a very real way of loving. Don't despise it or tire of it; such simple acts have always been and still are real steps on the way into the simple loving of God.

One of the great developments of this way has been the 'hesychast' prayer, or 'prayer of the heart' developed in the Eastern Orthodox churches from the sixth century, and more particularly between the tenth and fourteenth. This has taught a way of concentration in prayer round the repetition of the name of Jesus. The Jesus prayer is not an end in itself, but a way into a steady loving, or prayer of the heart – a way to respond to the infinite wonder of God and to a prayer of quiet – in Greek, hesychast. The Orthodox masters of the spiritual life found that the longer phrase, 'Lord Jesus Christ, Son of God, have mercy on me' could give both rhythm and content to the prayer. It was found too that the rhythm could be further developed by praying in time with breathing. This is quite simple with practice, and you can find for yourself how effective this can be. With concentration this can lead to a loving and looking at Jesus; it can help to make an actual relationship with him. This kind of prayer comes back quite easily and naturally at odd moments of waiting in life, and so helps to build up that relationship.

These points of rhythm and phrase are, of course, common to many ways of praying across the world and its religions. The distinctiveness of the Jesus prayer is that it concentrates on the particular person of Jesus and so has specific content. It opens the way to a relationship with the living personal God, who can draw us out of ourselves, not in an impersonal passivity, but into an active personal love for him. At the same time Jesus will never let us forget our neighbour. These points are all worth remembering. Christian writers who have taught the use of attention to the body, to posture, to breathing, have always seen these as a means to an end, the end of attention to God and to his concerns for his children. Those who seek to combine the techniques of Eastern religion with Christianity must ask themselves very carefully whether attention to body posture, to breathing and so on, are directed towards God and his will as revealed in Jesus, and his care for others, or whether really they are directed towards their own well-being.

The name of Jesus very obviously has had a central place in the prayer of loving for Christians of a wide variety of traditions. Our hymn books bear witness to the attraction of the name of Jesus both before and after the Reformation. Our books contain several versions derived from the medieval office hymn 'Jesu dulcis memoria'. In the eighteenth century they had the evangelical John Newton's 'How sweet the name of Jesus sounds', and from the nineteenth century the Quaker J. G. Whittier's 'Immortal love for ever full', bears witness to the repetition of the name from the nursery to the deathbed. They also remind us that behind the outward lips must be love which alone 'comprehendeth love'.

In the Christian tradition of loving God there has always been a looking through the words and actions of Jesus to the love beyond. Yet the words and action and the person of Jesus are not dispensable; they tell us that God is personal, that he does make himself known in a definite way and a definite demand in this world. So Whittier echoes the New Testament when he says 'Alone O love ineffable, thy saving name is given.' It is a fact that for some people all their loving of God is centred in Jesus, and not least in his cross. This need not be limiting, but illuminating.

One of the richest examples of this love for Jesus is given in the *Revelations of Divine Love* of Mother Julian of Norwich, the fourteenth-century recluse, who left us an account of the series of visions she had during an illness, together with the understanding which came to her over the next twenty years. Her visions were formed round the cross which was held near her, as she appeared to be at the point of death. Over the years she saw more and more through these, God's love embracing the world 'like a hazel nut for smallness', as one of her phrases puts it, and embracing the world's failures on the cross so that 'his wounds are worships' as another phrase has it. This leads her to the confident refrain 'all shall be well, and all shall be very well'. Just as the Jesus prayer can come to the lips and minds as we wait at a bus stop, so the pictures and refrain of Mother Julian can come to us in times when life seems sick, or vast, or a failure.

An anonymous contemporary of Julian's, probably a priest in the East Midlands, has left us help in looking and loving in a further direction in *The Cloud of Unknowing*. The modern translation by C. F. Wolters in the Penguin Classics has made this book and the *Revelations* of Mother Julian very accessible to modern readers. The anonymous author of *The Cloud of Unknowing* clearly writes within a relationship with Christ, but helps us to look through and beyond this. He wrote in a time when prayer was largely vocal prayer, and pleads to reduce all prayer to the shortest acts, He suggests the repetition of such words as 'sin' or 'out' to beat down the 'dark cloud of forgetting' or distraction. He suggests the simple words of 'God' or 'love' as short arrows of love into the 'cloud of unknowing' which is our perspective of the glory of God. Love must find a way into that glory in the end. 'By love may he be gotten, but not by knowing', the author says. This tallies with what we have found on the way of attention to God by short repeated acts. The words drop away, but we still have to make short bursts of loving and longing and looking. The 'dark cloud of unknowing' is a very fair description of the outlook of that longing. For some the cloud breaks, at least for moments; for others it never appears to do so in this life apparently. The writer is not unduly concerned about this; it is the loving that finds God rather than the looking.

So say other writers on prayer in the same vein. John of the Cross gives the final part of his poetical picture of the spiritual life the title of 'The Living Flame of Love'. Jan van Ruysbroek, the fourteenth-century Flemish writer gave his great book the title of *The Spiritual Espousals* to show that this relationship, for all its illumination is at the same time personal. There are conditions for this illumination. It is seen that the longest section of Ruysbroek's book is the central one, the way of yearning, the way through to the final stage of illumination. The way of yearning is the way to loving.

'By love may he be gotten and not by knowing' writes the author of the *Cloud of Unknowing*, and we may put alongside this the first epistle of St John 'we love because he first loved us'. We can be sure that God holds us in love all the time. This may give us the confidence to try loving God using our human experience of love. The ground base of thankfulness can help to build up this confidence and strengthen our trust, and lead to great delight in God. We may begin to gain the confidence that all is not too good to be true; we are not kidding ourselves. So we can let ourselves go to 'wonder, love and praise'.

We may find it a help to let ourselves go by responding in our physical position in various ways. At times we may do this best in a relaxed sitting position, then we may want to move to a more positive attitude, perhaps by standing, fixing our eyes on an object or a picture or a blank wall. It is not that attention to a living God can be regarded as emptiness, but as to be filled with his presence. Then we may value a return to kneeling, or more likely to prostration, to let ourselves go to God lying flat out, on the floor or on a bed.

The way we love God is rightly a very personal matter,

spiritually and physically. These suggestions may seem too obvious to some, but very odd to others. We must remember, however, that we are human beings, and that God has made himself supremely knowable in the human life of Jesus. He knows our need to express our love in our human body and attitudes. At the same time we need to be modest about them, and not think they are ends in themselves – the end is a meeting of the whole person with a personal God.

This will vary, therefore, from person to person, and for most of us from time to time. We will approach it from different directions at different stages. We may find ourselves looking at different aspects of love at different times, but we can let that be. God is to be loved in all sorts of ways. It is as simple and as rich as that; we shall always find there is more to be discovered in loving God, and yet we shall find more amazing simplicity and humility in that love. Our Lord is very homely, as Mother Julian discovered.

Love is the end of prayer and also its beginning, so we can content ourselves when our prayer is not always sustained at the level of contemplation, but becomes again dependent on words and on reading. We can also content ourselves when we find we have very real responsibilities in intercession, or in thanksgiving and penitence. Other people will soon know if we fail in these responsibilities, but these very parts of prayer will be all the deeper if we remember that they are part of loving God and our neighbour in and for him. We shall also find that we can sustain them and understand these kinds of prayer better if we treat them as opportunities for loving God for himself.

We often find ourselves moving backwards and forwards in prayer, and we must not be alarmed by this. In prayer we may find the chance or the urge to stop and to love God, and it is worth taking this. It may arise when we are thinking about concerns for others, or being thankful about something or seeing that we need to be sorry. When you find yourself looking into the depth and loving what you see, give yourself to it. Then when the attention and spontaneity recedes, be ready to do some more reading or thinking about God, or the needs of others or what we ought to be doing. In that way we shall find ourselves carried further and deeper into the give and take of love with God. We have to learn to pass freely from the one to the other. There may be momentary regrets, but there should be a fundamental trust and zest, for the exchange of love gives point and joy to every activity. As time goes on it should simplify and unify our life; so that we find ourselves saying or thinking, in work or in prayer, 'of course, this makes sense'. 'We love, because he first loved us.' 'By love may he be gotten, but not by knowing.' So in the end we can echo the old lyric –

> To those who fall how kind thou art,
> How good to those who seek!
> But what to those who find? Ah this
> Nor tongue, nor pen can show.

SOME HELPFUL BOOKS

For finding the way in, three short books by contemporary guides:

Mark Gibbard, *Why Pray?*, SCM Press 1970
Michael Hollings, *Day by Day*, Mayhew-McCrimmon 1972
Anthony Bloom, *School for Prayer*, Darton, Longman & Todd 1970

For a further look, one very readable longer book and three shorter ones, the last of especial significance:

J. Neville Ward, *The Use of Praying*, Epworth 1968
Harry Williams, *Becoming What I am*, Darton, Longman & Todd 1977
Mark Gibbard, *Prayer and Contemplation*, Mowbray 1976
Monica Furlong, *Contemplating Now*, Hodder & Stoughton 1971

These point back to the well-marked road of Christian prayer. Some of the most notable books are made available for us now in modern versions – from England in the fourteenth century, Spain in the sixteenth century, France in the eighteenth century and Russia in the nineteenth century:

The Cloud of Unknowing, Penguin Books 1961
Mother Julian of Norwich, *Revelations of Divine Love*, Penguin Books 1966
St John of the Cross, *Complete Works*, ed. A. Peers, Anthony Clarke 1953
St Teresa, *The Interior Castle*, ed. A. Peers, Sheed & Ward 1974
The Way of Perfection, Sheed & Ward 1977

J. P. de Caussade, *Self-abandonment to Divine Providence*, Burns & Oates 1953, Fontana edition 1971
J. N. Grou, *How to Pray*, James Clarke 1955
R. M. French (ed.), *The Way of a Pilgrim*, Seabury Press 1968

A great translator of the past into the twentieth century:
Evelyn Underhill, *The Mystics of the Church*, James Clarke 1925
On the Love of God (an anthology of her own writings), Mowbray 1976

Much contemporary spirituality comes through France, particularly through the Little Brothers of Charles de Foucauld:
René Voillaume, *Brothers of Men*, Darton, Longman & Todd 1966
Faith and Contemplation, Darton, Longman & Todd 1974
Carlo Carretto, *Letters from the Desert*, Darton, Longman & Todd 1971
In Search of the Beyond, Darton, Longman & Todd 1975
and the remarkable priest who has opened up new ways of praying from life in his reflections and meditations:
Michel Quoist, *Prayers of Life*, Gill & Macmillan 1963
The Christian Response, Gill & Macmillan 1965
Meet Christ and Live, Gill & Macmillan 1962

This way has been taken up in England:
Rex Chapman, *A Kind of Praying*, SCM Press 1970
The Cry of the Spirit, SCM Press 1974
Another way in from the international scene:
Dag Hammarskjöld, *Markings*, Faber & Faber 1964.